S. Hrg. 114–211

THE FUTURE OF WARFARE

HEARING

BEFORE THE

COMMITTEE ON ARMED SERVICES
UNITED STATES SENATE

ONE HUNDRED FOURTEENTH CONGRESS

FIRST SESSION

NOVEMBER 3, 2015

Printed for the use of the Committee on Armed Services

Available via the World Wide Web: http://www.fdsys.gov/

U.S. GOVERNMENT PUBLISHING OFFICE

99–570 PDF   WASHINGTON : 2016

(II)

CONTENTS

NOVEMBER 3, 2015

THE FUTURE OF WARFARE

TUESDAY, NOVEMBER 3, 2015

U.S. SENATE,
COMMITTEE ON ARMED SERVICES,
Washington, D.C.

The committee met, pursuant to notice, at 9:27 a.m. in Room SD-G50, Dirksen Senate Office Building, Hon. John McCain (chairman) presiding.

Committee Members Present: Senators McCain [presiding], Inhofe, Sessions, Wicker, Ayotte, Fischer, Cotton, Rounds, Ernst, Tillis, Sullivan, Reed, Nelson, McCaskill, Manchin, Shaheen, Gillibrand, Blumenthal, Donnelly, Hirono, Kaine, and King.

OPENING STATEMENT OF SENATOR JOHN McCAIN, CHAIRMAN

Chairman MCCAIN. Well, good morning. The committee meets this morning to consider the future of warfare. This hearing builds on a series of hearings this committee is conducting to discuss our current geopolitical challenges, examine the ability of our defense enterprise to meet these challenges, and identify what reforms are necessary to ensure that we have the most agile, innovative, and effective military and defense organization possible.

Today we focus on the future, what features will define the battlefields of tomorrow, what technologies and methods of employing them our future warfighters will require, and what we must do to reform our defense institutions to function and adapt closer to the need of innovation than the speed of bureaucracy.

We are fortunate to have a distinguished panel of witnesses this morning who will present their views on how to reimagine and reshape our military for the future. General Keith Alexander, former Commander of U.S. Cyber Command and Director of the National Security Agency, an outstanding leader. Mr. Bryan Clark, Senior Fellow at the Center for Strategic and Budgetary Assessments. Mr. Paul Scharre, a Senior Fellow and Director of the 20YY Warfare Initiative at the Center for a New American Security. Dr. Peter Singer, Strategist and Senior Fellow at the New America Foundation.

The witnesses who have testified before this committee continue to warn that the current global threat environment is the most challenging, complex, and uncertain in 70 years. But what is truly disturbing is that as we look to the future, the trends that are making the world more dangerous seem likely to persist and intensify.

Many of our adversaries are investing billions of dollars into reshaping their militaries and developing technologies to counter and thwart America's military advantages. At the same time, the speed of globalization and commercialization means that advanced disruptive technologies are increasingly available to rival militaries, terrorist groups, and other non-state actors. Add to that the harm caused by the Budget Control Act and sequestration, and we are now facing the dual problem of a quantitative and qualitative erosion of our military edge.

Reversing this trend certainly requires greater military capacity. There is still a lot of truth in the old adage that quantity has a quality all its own. That said, simply buying more of what we have now is insufficient. That is not how we will preserve our military technological advantage or win our future wars. Our enemies are not just investing in new defense technologies, they are investing in strategies to counter America's traditional military strengths asymmetrically through cyber, hybrid warfare, and anti-access and area denial capabilities. Doing more of the same simply plays into our adversaries' hands.

As the National Defense Panel concluded, quote, "maintaining the operational and technological edge of our armed forces requires sustained and targeted investment." I want to emphasize "targeted." We are witnessing rapid technological advancement in areas such as cyber and space capabilities, robotics, and unmanned systems, miniaturization, and directed energy, hypersonics, and data analytics. This is not science fiction. It is happening right now and we better understand the implications of these changes for the future of warfare because we know our adversaries are working overtime to do so.

This is a major defense acquisition challenge because these kinds of disruptive technologies are being developed more by non-traditional commercial companies than traditional defense industry. Indeed, the top four U.S. defense contractors combined spend only 27 percent of what Google does annually on research and development, and yet the defense acquisition system all too often serves to repel rather than attract producers of disruptive new technologies. Leading commercial companies are innovating on an 18-month cycle, but the Department of Defense is stuck on 18-year cycles. This is a recipe for failure and fixing this problem must continue to be a top priority for this committee's acquisition reform efforts.

It is not enough, however, just to acquire new technologies. We must also devise entirely new ways to employ them. It would be a failure of imagination merely to try to conform emerging defense technologies to how we operate and fight today. Ultimately, we must recognize the radical potential that these capabilities possess and shape new ways of operating and fighting around these new technologies.

The classic example is the tank prior to World War II. At the time, all the major powers had tanks, but they could only imagine them as mobile artillery or armored cavalry. It as the Germans who first understood that a tank is a tank, and they built entirely new operational concepts around it and realized its true potential.

Similarly, the United States Navy in the 1930's adapted itself despite fervent opposition at times, both internal and external, from a force built around a battleship to one organized around carrier aviation. Key military leaders at that time anticipated the opportunities that aviation presented, developed novel ways to fight with aircraft at sea, and prepared our Nation to wage and win a new type of naval warfare.

We face similar challenges now. Instead of thinking about how cyber or unmanned systems or other new technologies can simply enable us to do things we are already doing now, we must discern the real potential of these capabilities, both how they may be used against us and how they should be used by us. Then we must rethink and reimagine and reshape our military around these disruptive new technologies. That is the only way we will sustain our qualitative military edge.

This will require tough choices. Prioritizing for the future will not always be popular in all quarters of the defense establishment. Advocates for the status quo will likely resist change. But these are the choices we must make to ensure that our military will be ready to deter and, if necessary, fight and win our future wars.

I look forward to the testimony of our witnesses.

Senator Reed?

STATEMENT OF SENATOR JACK REED

Senator REED. Well, thank you very much, Mr. Chairman.

Let me join you in thanking our witnesses for their willingness to appear today to provide their thoughts on the future of warfare and how it may shape the organization of and the investments in our military going forward. Each of you has contributed to our national discussion on these issues. I look forward to your testimony. Thank you, gentlemen.

A central theme of last week's hearing, one that I suspect will continue today, is the steady erosion of U.S. technological superiority and the need for a so-called third offset strategy to recapture a distinct qualitative advantage over our adversaries in operationally critical areas. The presumption that the decades' long technological superiority enjoyed by the United States and our allies will continue into the future may no longer be valid, as near peer competitors have learned from our past success and made advancements of their own, particularly in the areas of precision and long-range strike, anti-access/area denial, space, and cyber. This diffusion of technology has even impacted our advantages over non-state groups like ISIL [Islamic State of Iraq and the Levant] and al Qaeda who are increasingly able to acquire and employ tools, including drones and satellite communications equipment which would have been unthinkable only a few years ago.

As Deputy Secretary of Defense Bob Work told students at the National Defense University last year, as any good student of Clausewitz knows, the fundamental nature of war is an interactive clash, a two-sided duel, action followed by reaction. While the United States fought two lengthy wars, the rest of the world did not sit idly. They saw what our advantages were back in 1991's Desert Storm and they studied them and they set about devising ways to compete. He continued, our forces face the very real possibility of arriving in a future combat theater and finding themselves facing an arsenal of advanced disruptive technologies that could turn our previous technological advantage on its head where our armed forces no longer have uncontested theater access or unfettered operational freedom of maneuver.

Underlying these challenges are several technological trends that are reshaping the future of warfare. Global investment, notably by the commercial sector, in research and innovation is far outpacing the research and development budgets of the DOD [Department of Defense] and the U.S. Government as a whole. To compete, we will have to develop better acquisition hiring policies, harness this trend to incentivize some of those talented scientists and engineers in the U.S. private sector to work with us. We will have to protect the military and civilian research programs, laboratories, and agencies that are driving innovation that will shape our future military capabilities. The pace of technological change is accelerating, but DOD processes seem to be slower and more bureaucratic than ever. We need a 21st century defense enterprise to keep up, and I hope this is a key theme in the committee's efforts at defense reform being led by the chairman.

Beyond acquisition reform, this includes the development of new military concepts of operations that, for example, deal with complex robotic systems, new rules of engagement for the expanding cyber battlefield, new regulations to smartly deal with expanded use of things like nanotechnology, artificial intelligence, or biotechnology, and a new attitude both in the Pentagon and in Congress that encourages the informed risk taking and innovation that is characteristic of the people and companies that are shaping the future.

I welcome the witnesses' thoughts and suggestions on these issues, and I look forward to the testimony. Thank you, Mr. Chairman.

Chairman McCAIN. Thank you.

General Alexander, welcome.

STATEMENT OF GENERAL KEITH B. ALEXANDER, USA, RET., FORMER COMMANDER, U.S. CYBER COMMAND AND FORMER DIRECTOR, NATIONAL SECURITY AGENCY

General ALEXANDER. Thank you, sir. Chairman McCain, Ranking Member Reed, distinguished members of the committee, I would like to talk briefly about what you have addressed in your opening statement, Chairman, about where technology is going and what this means to the future of warfare. I am going to do this rather quickly.

I submitted a statement for the record and would ask that that be put on the record.

Chairman McCAIN. All witness statements will be made a permanent part of the record.

General ALEXANDER. Thank you, Chairman.

When you look at the rate of change of technology, what you brought up in terms of the cycle of where we are with the DOD acquisition system and where industry is, 18 years, versus 18 months, it is unacceptable especially when we look at cybersecurity. When you think about the rate of change for cybersecurity, it is doubling every 2 years. So that means that the kids that are in college today, what they learn in their freshman year—half of it is outdated by their junior year. When you think about the volume of information that is being created, the unique volume of information, it is about 7 exabytes. What that means is we are going to create more unique information this year than the last 5,000 years combined. When you think about the staggering rate of that change of information and where it is going, and then you look at on the civilian side, the top 10 in-demand jobs now did not exist 10 years ago. So that means we are teaching students for jobs that do not exist, using technology that has not been created to solve problems we do not even know are problems.

But there is tremendous good that is going to come out of this in terms of the future of warfare and health care and saving money for our taxpayers in the energy market and others. When you look at just the revolution that is going to go on in the energy sector and how we can stabilize our Nation and other nations' energy sector and not waste billions of dollars in fuel costs a year, this is a huge opportunity for our Nation.

But with that opportunity comes tremendous vulnerability, and when you think about what the Defense Department is required to do, it rests on that civilian infrastructure. It rests on the energy sector, the communications infrastructure, and all of the other communications that are intertwined. Our Nation, in order to execute warfare, depends on that being there. It is not secure. Tremendous vulnerabilities.

I will just hit some highlights of what I think we are going to face over the next several years. You only need to look back at what happened in Estonia in 2007, first a distributed denial of service attack; 2008, a distributed denial of service attack. Both of those were by Russian hackers. I learned this from my daughter to put footnotes around when she said a dirty word, but I will use "Russian hackers." These are FSB [Federal Security Service]. They are going after our Nation. In 2007, it was Estonia. In 2008, it was Georgia uniquely timed to Russian troops entering into Georgia. As you know, Chairman, 2008 in October is when we found malware on the Defense Department's networks. If you jump to 2012, we saw a series of distributed denial of service attacks against our Nation's financial systems, largely attributed to Iran. It was preceded by a destructive attack against Saudi Aramco that destroyed the data on over 30,000 systems. So from 2012 August when that attack occurred to 2013, 350 attacks against our Nation's financial infrastructure.

Now, when you jump forward to where we are today with what has happened to Target, Home Depot, Sony, and you look at what hit other countries, you are seeing that those nations who disagree with us are looking at ways to come at us using the full spectrum of power, diplomatic, political, economic, military, and within military, the easiest form for at least Russia and Iran, has been cyber. Now when you look at what is going on around the world today, you can see that what is going on in Syria, if we have a disagreement with Russia, or if the Iran deal goes bad, or if we do not have a meeting of the mind on the Ukraine, or something pops up in North Korea, I expect these countries will come back at us with cyber attacks, and they can say not our guys. It is an asymmetric way of hitting our country and cause tremendous damage. Our Nation is not ready for these types of attacks across the board.

I think the cyber legislation that was brought forward takes us a great step down the road, but I think there is more that needs to be done. Within the Defense Department, only the Defense Department can defend this Nation in cyber. Homeland Security can set standards, but when our Nation is under attack, the U.S. Cyber Command, NSA [National Security Agency], FBI [Federal Bureau of Investigation]—those are the ones who are going to be the first responders.

So let us look at what happened to Sony and use that as a case example to end my opening statement, Chairman.

When Sony was hit—everybody can say, well, that is not critical infrastructure. I have got it. But when Sony was attacked, we would not allow as a Government Sony to attack back against North Korea. The reason is if Sony were to attack back, it could start a bigger war on the Korean peninsula. That is the responsibility of governments. But if Sony is not allowed to attack back, then who does that for Sony? That is where our Government steps in. That is where our Defense Department is, and that is what we are needed for. But we cannot see Sony's networks, and I am not advocating for the Government to be in all the networks.

What I would advocate for is like a radar system. When a company or a sector is being hit, that they can tell the Government at large I am being attacked.

Now, two things have to occur in order to do that. Those companies need to up their game in cybersecurity and understand what is going on, and they need to, much like a radar system, be able to tell the Government something is going on. Then the Government can determine what to do. All of this has to occur at network speed. It is not a place where you can have someone in the loop making a decision. Chairman, it is analogous to doing nuclear exchange where we are racing down the road building powerpoints to brief the White House on the next step when the missiles come in 30 minutes and the briefings come in 30 hours. In cyberspace, to go halfway around the world takes 67 milliseconds. That is your decision space. It does not provide any opportunity for us to miscalculate in this area.

When you think about what those who wish us harm want to do, if I were a bad guy—I am a good guy, Chairman, I believe. If I were a bad guy, I would look at this as a military campaign and say how do I want to attack our financial sector, our energy sector, and our Government. I believe those who want to do us harm can do that much like what happened in 2012 but this time with more destructive tools against our energy sector and against our financial sector. If that happens the cost to our Nation would be measured in the trillions.

So where do we need to go? I think that is one of the things, Chairman, that we ought to discuss, where we go in this area, how we set up and organize within the Government and set the rules of engagement and get things right, train our troops across the board, and partner with industry. We have got to do both. We need industry to tells us what is going on, but the Government has got to be there to protect industry. I am not an advocate of us pushing money to industry for them to go fix their problem. I am advocate for industry upping their game and having the capability to tell the Government that something is going on.

These are areas that—you know, I like to really talk about what is going on in this domain. When you look at it and the Internet, our Nation is the one who created the Internet. We were the first to do this. We ought to be the first to secure it.

Thank you, Chairman.

[The prepared statement of General Alexander follows:]

PREPARED STATEMENT OF GEN (RET) KEITH B. ALEXANDER*

Chairman McCain, Ranking Member Reed, Members of the Committee: thank you for inviting me to discuss the future of warfare with you all today and, specifically, to engage in a dialogue with this Committee about two of the most pressing threats facing our Nation: (1) the threat from terrorist groups with global reach and ambitions; and (2) the threat from criminal syndicates and nation-states in cyberspace. I plan to talk candidly about these topics and give you a sense of where I think we are headed and what we might do to mitigate the very serious risks and threats we face as a nation.

I want to thank you, Mr. Chairman, for taking the time to look at the major issues facing the Department of Defense and how we might architect the Department and our military services as we face evolving threats in this new environment. The efforts both you and the Ranking Member have made in this area will help ensure the security of our going forward and will help us keep faith with the men and women who serve our country with pride and honor in the far reaches of the globe.

Before we turn to the future of warfare, it is important to discuss some of the significant changes going on in the hugely challenging global environment we find ourselves in today. In my mind, this discussion is critically important because it frames the way we need to think about future conflicts and how we might shape the Defense Department and our military services to be prepared for these conflicts.

We live in amazing, challenging, and threatening times. Around the world, we see conflicts or situations that could easily spiral out of control, dramatically affecting our national security. Indeed, in many places, this process has potentially already begun. From the longstanding homeland threat posed by al Qaeda core and its affiliates around the world, to the growth of a potential terrorist state in the lands of Iraq and Syria, and the increasing role of Hizballah and Hamas in various conflict zones, just to name a few, the threat of terrorism is on the rise. Even more troubling, major nation-states continue to behave in ways that seek to challenge the United States and intimidate our allies.

China continues to experience tremendous economic difficulties that drive their need to steal intellectual property and strengthen their stance in the South China Sea. Russia's intervention in Ukraine and in the Syrian conflict are just the start of a potential series of actions that seek to reshape the international environment in ways that do not reflect America's interests. A number of key allies and other important states face the very real threat of internal dissent and potential collapse. These regional conflicts and the surge of terrorist activities point to an uncertain future, with tremendous potential impact on our Nation.

Moreover, in the cyber realm, we also see threats increasing. Whether it is the growing spread of nation-state espionage, including hacks against government systems and the rampant theft of core U.S. intellectual property from our companies, or financial crime conducted by criminal syndicates and nation-state sponsored groups, or the very real threat of destructive cyber attacks against critical infrastructure companies, we are seeing a rapid increase of challenges in this domain also.

The evolution of computers and networks, the growing challenges to network and cyber security, and underlying concerns about civil liberties and privacy greatly complicate these areas. I am deeply concerned that our current cybersecurity strategy is incomplete at best and is further complicated by many of these issues.

---

*Gen. (Ret) Keith Alexander is the former Director of the National Security Agency and former Commander, United States Cyber Command. He currently serves as the President and CEO of IronNet Cybersecurity, a startup technology company headquartered in the Washington, DC metropolitan region.

I would like to start first with technology, then turn to terrorism, and finally briefly discuss how we might work to improve military readiness in these areas.

Technology is an area of rapid and dramatic change and growth, with processing capacity doubling every two years under Moore's law.[1] Moreover, Cisco estimates that annual global IP [Internet Protocol] network traffic will exceed one zettabyte by the end of 2016 (or nearly 1 billion gigabytes per month), and will nearly double to two zettabytes per year by 2019.[2] This means that global Internet traffic in 2019 will be approximately 66 times the volume of the entire global Internet traffic in 2005.[3] Around the world, the number of devices connected to IP networks will be more than three times the global population by 2019.[4]

While former Secretary of Education Richard Riley's prediction in the early 2000s about the job change across the economy may not have been exactly right, it certainly seems to me that his point is spot on when it comes to technology: namely, that many of the specific jobs available in technology today didn't even exist a decade ago; indeed, the notion, attributed to Riley, that "we are training young people for jobs that don't even exist yet, to use technology that hasn't been created yet, to solve problems that we don't even know are problems yet" seems clearly right.[5] Others have noted that for the first time in history, we have four generations working side-by-side: the "write me," "call me," "email me," and "text me" generations.[6] Today, we think and talk about communications and human interaction fundamentally differently. We talk about "hanging out"—not in person, but online via Google; we talk about swiping, not to steal something, but to look for a mate on Tinder. Indeed, any person with access to Google today has better access to information than the President of the United States did 20 years ago. Some have suggested that by 2049, a $1,000 computer will exceed the computational capabilities of the entire human race.[7]

These changes are stunning and, in my view, form the foundation for other great revolutions. For example, nanotechnology is utilizing these data advances to make amazing progress. In June of 2014, I had a chance to see the improvements IBM is making in addressing brain cancer by partnering with the Genome Center in New York City. The prognosis on brain cancer radiation treatment that used to take nearly a month for a panel of oncologists can now be done in minutes with computer analytics.

As such, technological change presents tremendous opportunities. But with these tremendous opportunities come tremendous vulnerabilities. From my perspective, there are four major threats in the cyber domain: cyber attack, cyber espionage, cyber theft of intellectual property, and criminal activity. In 2014, the Center for Strategic and International Studies estimated the worldwide loss from cybercrime to be $445 billion annually.[8] While this number seeks to account for the theft of intellectual property, in my view, the value of theft of intellectual property from American industry is significantly greater than accounted for in this study and, in fact, represents the single greatest transfer of wealth in history.

At the same time, the potential for actual cyber attacks also represents a major threat to our national security. Both the scope and nature of this threat is growing, as is the probability of increasing disruptive and destructive attacks. Specifically, since the 2007 attacks against Estonia, the pace and nature of cyber attacks has grown. In 2008, we had the attacks against Georgia and the discovery of agent.btz malware in U.S. military systems. In 2012, we learned of the first publicly disclosed destructive attack against Saudi Aramco, where data on approximately 30,000 computers was destroyed, followed soon there after by a similar attack on Qatari

---

[1] See Annie Sneed, *Moore's Law Keeps Going, Defying Expectations,* Scientific American (May 14, 2015) *available online at <http://www.scientificamerican.com/article/moore-s-law-keeps-going-defying-expectations/>.*

[2] See Cisco, *The Zettabyte Era—Trends and Analysis* (May 2015), available online at *<http://www.cisco.com/c/en/us/solutions/collateral/service-provider/visual-networking-index-vni/VNI_Hyperconnectivity_WP.html>*

[3] *Id.*

[4] *Id.*

[5] See Steve Gunderson, et al., THE JOBS REVOLUTION: CHANGING HOW AMERICA WORKS, 58–60 (2004); David Tritelli, *From the Editor,* Liberal Education, vol. 9, no. 1 (Winter 2009), available online at *<https://www.aacu.org/publications-research/periodicals/editor-56>.*

[6] *Cf., e.g.,* Mareisha Winters, *Write Me, Call Me, Text Me: Generational Differences in the Workplace,* Let's Talk About Work (Aug. 15, 2012), available online at *<http://www.letstalk aboutwork.tv/write-me-call-me-text-me-generational-differences-workplace/>.*

[7] See Ray Kurzweil, *The Law of Accelerating Returns* (March 7, 2001), available online at *<http://www.kurzweilai.net/the-law-of-accelerating-returns>.*

[8] *See* Center for Strategic and International Studies, *Net Losses: Estimating the Global Cost of Cybercrime* (May 2014), available online at *<http://csis.org/files/attachments/140609_rp_economic_impact_cybercrime_report.pdf>.*

RasGas. Between 2012 and 2014, we saw large-scale distributed denial of service attacks on U.S. bank websites. We have all heard about the potential impact of the Havex and BlackEnergy malware on industrial control systems in the energy industry. We also see cyber threats from criminal actors, although these are largely focused on theft, including of customer data, at places like Target and Home Depot.

While many of these hacks might be achieved with relative ease, most of the prominent events that we discussed have involved very sophisticated attackers using unique skill sets, clearly suggesting that there is some measure or potential of nation-state involvement or sponsorship.

Having now talked about the cyber threat, I like to turn back to the terrorism threat, which we discussed briefly earlier and then get into how we might think about some of these issues going forward.

On terrorism, just a few key points. There has been a massive increase in global terrorist acts and deaths from terrorism in recent years. According to State Department statistics, between 2012 and 2013, we saw a 43% increase in terrorist attacks worldwide and 61% increase in people killed as a result of terrorism. [9] Between 2013 and 2014, we saw another 39% increase in attacks and an 83% increase in deaths, which represents a nearly tripling of deaths in just two years. [10]

When you combine these statistics with the issues we discussed briefly before: the permissive environments created by government collapse in countries like Yemen and Libya, ISIS [Islamic State of Iraq and Syria] control of territory between the lands of Iraq and Syria, increased Iranian support for proxy group like Hizballah and Shia militias in Iraq, continued interest by core al Qaeda and its affiliates like AQAP [Al-Qaeda in the Arabian Peninsula] in homeland attacks, and the increasing pace of conflicts that continues to potentially destabilize countries in the Middle East, North Africa and elsewhere, we see a very challenging environment for America's national security and a clearly increasing terrorist threat.

Having discussed the challenges facing us in both the cyber and terrorism environments, I would like to also briefly talk about key areas we need to change within the Defense Department to counter these asymmetric threats.

When I retired in April 2014, I believed I could "continue the mission" by helping the private sector better protect themselves with better cybersecurity solutions. I believe there is much to be done to bring commercial cybersecurity to the "right" standard and my experience, to date, is that business leaders are working these issues hard. In building a comprehensive approach to cybersecurity, we need to build a foundational framework that will give us the opportunity to provide game-changing new defensive capabilities to the private sector.

More importantly, commercial and private entities cannot defend themselves alone against nation-state attacks nor nation-state-like attacks in cyberspace. We do not want them to "fire" back. The U.S. Government is the only one that can and should "fire" back. That is, it is the government's job to defend this country in cyberspace from the type of destructive attacks that hit Sony and the disruptive attacks that hit Wall Street from August 2012 to April 2013. Truth be told, our Nation simply is not prepared for these events, at least at this time.

To resolve this problem, we need cyber legislation that provides clear authority and liability protection to incentivize information sharing. Thank you for the work all of you have done in passing the cyber legislation. However, that legislation needs to ensure the government can do its job of defending our Nation at network speed, because that is the speed of these attacks. We also need industry to be able to "tell" the government when they are under attack, at network speed, and the appropriate entities in government should receive this information at network speed, *without delay*. Our Nation will depend on that capability and speed in the next cyber engagement we face.

In particular, for the Department of Defense, this means that DOD needs to receive information—directly and at network speed—that will help it protect the Nation. DHS [Department of Homeland Security] and other entities can receive this

[9] *Compare* U.S. State Department, COUNTRY REPORTS ON TERRORISM 2012, National Consortium for the Study of Terrorism and Responses to Terrorism: *Annex of Statistical Information* (2013), available online at <http://www.state.gov/j/ct/rls/crt/2012/210017.htm> (6771 attacks; 11098 fatalities) *with* U.S. State Department, COUNTRY REPORTS ON TERRORISM 2013, National Consortium for the Study of Terrorism and Responses to Terrorism: *Annex of Statistical Information* (2014), available online at <http://www.state.gov/j/ct/rls/crt/2013/224831.htm> (9707 attacks; 17891 fatalities)

[10] *Id.; compare also* COUNTRY REPORTS ON TERRORISM 2013 (9707 attacks; 17891 fatalities) *with* U.S. State Department, COUNTRY REPORTS ON TERRORISM 2014, National Consortium for the Study of Terrorism and Responses to Terrorism: *Annex of Statistical Information* (2015), available online at <http://www.state.gov/j/ct/rls/crt/2014/239416.htm> (13463 attacks;32727 fatalities).

information at the same time, but information relevant to the defense of this country should not be delayed by another department or agency. I know that the legislation has a range of provisions on this issue, some that provide flexibility, and others that route information through particular paths. It is critical that as the two Houses confer on the final bill, members should keep in mind the critical importance of speed and flexibility for protecting the Nation against threats that morph rapidly and in real-time.

As a consequence, we also need to build a complementary foundational framework within the Department of Defense. Most importantly, we need to have the right structure in place. As you know, during my tenure as Director of NSA, we worked closely within the Executive Branch and with this Committee to come up with the right structure and capability for U.S. Cyber Command. While these efforts have been successful and we have been able to bring a joint, combined arms approach together at Cyber Command, we now have an opportunity to go further. In my mind, some of the important concepts to consider include elevating U.S. Cyber Command to a Unified Command, providing it a consistent and increased set of funding authorities, investing in both people and technology enhancements, and preparing for what is an obviously more dangerous and rapidly changing environment. I believe our cyber investments should be analogous to and undertaken with the vigor and focus of the Manhattan project, and should involve both government and industry participants.

On both the cyber and terrorism fronts, we also need to make significant progress in thinking more clearly—both in strategic and tactical terms—about how to deal with the increasing scale and scope of asymmetric threats. In particular, the use of asymmetric capabilities by an increasingly broader array of actors, many of whom don't respond to typical state-to-state incentives, raises tough issues for our military. A lighter, faster, more responsive and agile set of forces, specifically aimed at the terrorism and cyber target sets, is critical. Similarly, providing more authority and flexibility to commanders in the field working in these areas is critical to taking advantage of a more flexible and responsive force.

In the end, while we have may significant progress in these areas in recent years, much more remains to be done and I look forward to providing you whatever assistance I can in your efforts going forward.

Thank you for your time and attention.

Chairman MCCAIN. Thank you very much, General. Mr. Clark?

STATEMENT OF BRYAN CLARK, SENIOR FELLOW, CENTER FOR STRATEGIC AND BUDGETARY ASSESSMENTS

Mr. CLARK. Good morning, Chairman. Chairman McCain, Ranking Member Reed, members of the committee, thank you for asking us to come here to testify today on this very important topic.

I wanted to highlight some elements from my written statement to get at the strategy we should be using to approach technology development and the Department of Defense to get at some of the trends that General Alexander and that yourself brought up earlier.

We have got a very dynamic security environment today, as we talked about in other sessions recently, and a very dynamic technology environment, as General Alexander highlighted. What that is doing is it is transitioning our several decades of military dominance that we have enjoyed since the Cold War into one of competition. So we are now going to have to compete to be able to maintain our warfighting edge against our likely adversaries.

To be able to maintain our technological edge, we need to have an effective strategy that goes after the kinds of enduring advantages that we need to be able to have to deterring the future. The last time we were faced with a situation like this, where we had a long-term competition against a single or a series of adversaries, was during the Cold War. During that period, we used several series of offset strategies that have been described by Secretary Work and others to be able to demonstrate to the Soviets that we would be able to hold them at risk, attack their targets at home, and attack their forces out in the field. These involved nuclear weapons initially with the new look of President Eisenhower's strategy in the 1950's, and it was followed later on with the strategies the Defense Department mounted with precision strike, stealth, and related capabilities, always keeping the Soviets on edge that they did not know if the U.S. was going to be able to effectively attack Soviet targets at will. That kept them probably from attacking our allies in Central Europe.

So these efforts were successful in large part, though, because we were able to identify the next phase in important mission areas such as strike and undersea warfare, develop capabilities that were going to be effective in that next phase of those warfare areas and establish an enduring advantage. So I will talk about a couple of examples.

So in one, in undersea warfare, at the beginning of the Cold War with the advent of the nuclear submarine, the U.S. realized that passive sonar and submarine quieting were going to be key features of undersea warfare going into the Cold War and developed those capabilities. As a result, we were able to maintain a dominant position in undersea warfare versus the Soviets for almost the entire Cold War, and that redounded to a benefit in terms of our strategic deterrence because we could protect our own ballistic missile submarines while threatening those of the Soviet Union, as well as giving us the ability to attack their attack submarines out at sea.

Another area would be stealth. So we saw later in the Cold War that Soviet radar systems were getting better and better. Those were being proliferated to their allies in the Warsaw Pact and elsewhere. So we started to develop stealth technologies and low probability of detection sensor systems that would need to be able to be effective against the kinds of sensors that the Soviets were developing. Those capabilities entered the force near the end of the Cold War, and we are all familiar with stealth being used in the Gulf War and then later gave us an advantage that still is benefiting the United States today in terms of the ability to strike targets at will almost anyplace on the globe. So several decades of benefit came from anticipating the next phase of warfare, developing the capabilities for it, and then moving into that next phase with an advantage that endures.

So once again now we find ourselves in a situation where we are geographically disadvantaged because our allies are far away and we have to project power in order to support them, and we are numerically disadvantaged because a lot of our potential adversaries like China have much bigger forces than our own.

So we need to, again, look at the approach we took in the Cold War of anticipating the next phase in some important warfare areas and important missions and then developing the capabilities to be effective in them. That should be the heart of our technology strategy, the offset strategies that we have been talking about. The third offset that Secretary Work talks about should be looking at the next phase of mission areas that we think are important to deterring the adversaries we are facing today.

So some of those shifts—I talk about them in detail in my written statement, but just to highlight the major shifts.

First of all, undersea warfare is likely to see a shift from listening for submarines with passive sonar and just quieting your submarines to one in which we use active sonar and non-acoustic methods to find submarines. That will mean our quiet submarines will not have the same benefit in terms of their survivability as they do today. We need to come up with new ways to counter detection using active systems, just as we do above the water to use jammers to counter radars. We will have to do the same thing under water probably.

In strike, we are going to see the continuation of the trend we saw towards stealth and low probability sensors that started during the Cold War but sort of went on hiatus with the Soviet Union's fall. So stealth and low probability detection sensors are going to be the de rigueur features of strike warfare going into the future.

In the EM spectrum [Electromagnetic Spectrum], we have been operating today with very high power systems, very detectable systems, and we are not going to be able to do that in the future. We will have to move to systems that are increasingly passive and low probability of detection. There are key technologies we need to develop in those areas.

Then last in air warfare, these sensor advancements are going to result in a situation where fast, small, maneuverable aircraft are going to no longer be as beneficial as large aircraft that can carry big sensors and large weapons payloads in air-to-air warfare.

So those are some key areas that we need to be able to take into our existing advantage and build upon in order to be successful against the adversaries we are likely to face in the future.

General Alexander brought up cyber and space. So cyberspace is obviously an area of competition today. Space is a big area of competition. But it looks like, given the policy choices that the United States has made and is likely to make in the future and our own dependence on both of those areas, it may not be that those are areas where we gain a significant military advantage. We may be faced with a situation where we just have to defend our current capabilities as opposed to being able to use those areas to asymmetrically go after our enemies. We may be forced into a defensive mode there.

So to be able to advance these technologies, we need to look at how we develop technology in the Defense Department. We have talked about and you talked about, Senator, the fact that we have an 18-month cycle in technology but an 18-year cycle in the Defense Department. There are some key ways that we need to drive the Defense Department to be able to develop technologies more quickly.

The first is operational concepts. Today we develop technologies absent a real idea of how we are going to use them, and we develop ways of fighting that do not take advantage of new technologies. We need to marry those two ideas up and get new operational concepts that leverage new technologies to be able to build requirements that drive the acquisition system towards new systems.

We also need to look at how we focus our technology investment. Today our technology investment is spread all over a large portfolio of areas instead of focused on those areas that are going to give us the greatest benefits strategically down the road. So we are watering all the flowers in hopes some of them will turn into trees, but in fact we need to focus on the ones that are most likely to turn into trees.

The last one is how do we develop requirements. Acquisition reform has been a big topic, I know, a big focus area of yours, and in the Department there is working going on as well. One key area that has not been addressed yet is the need to refine how to we develop requirements. When we develop the requirements for a new platform, we start from scratch every time we come up with a new airplane or ship or missile and define the requirements for it up front before we even start building the thing. Instead, we need to look at ways to build the requirements as we are prototyping technologies to get an idea of what requirements are going to be feasible. So how fast can it go for a reasonable cost? What is achievable in terms of schedule, and what is achievable in terms of the performance parameters of the particular weapon system? Those can be defined in large part by prototyping existing technologies and then building the requirements as you do that. That would be how a business might go about it, but in the Defense Department, we build requirements in isolation from any expectation as to how feasible it will be to deliver those requirements. So refining the requirements process will be a key feature of speeding up that introduction of new technologies.

So we have an opportunity here with our current technological capabilities, many of which are maturing in these mission areas that are really important, but we need to make some changes in order to leverage them to gain this enduring advantage that will take us into the future.

I look forward to your questions. Thank you.

[The prepared statement of Mr. Clark follows:]

PREPARED STATEMENT BY BRYAN CLARK

Chairman McCain, Senator Reed, thank you for inviting me to testify today on this important and timely subject. It is one we will have to address for the American military to continue credibly protecting our people, territory, allies, and interests. Without a comprehensive effort to sustain, and in some cases regain, our technological advantage, the U.S. military will have less ability to deter aggression and be compelled to fight more often to demonstrate American resolve. When they do fight, U.S. forces will be at a disadvantage against our enemies.

After almost three decades of military dominance following the fall of the Soviet Union, the United States is facing an era of increased competition. New technologies are levelling the playing field for rivals such as Russia, China, and the Islamic State seeking to overturn existing borders and security relationships. They are leveraging their proximity to U.S. allies and new military capabilities to pursue their objectives while increasing the risk for arriving U.S. forces. This may significantly raise the bar for American intervention while aggressors quietly accrete territory and influence at the expense of America's friends and allies.

This situation is clearly untenable. The U.S. Department of Defense (DOD) must do more than its current effort to develop plans that will produce new weapon systems in 10–15 years. It must take advantage of emerging technologies from DOD research labs as well as defense and commercial industry to rapidly field new capabilities in key missions such as undersea, strike, air, and electronic warfare that will impose costs on America's rivals and improve the capability of U.S. forces.

THE "THIRD OFFSET STRATEGY"

During the Cold War, U.S. forces mitigated their geographic separation from American allies and numerical disadvantages against the Soviets by deploying nuclear weapons in the 1950s and long-range precision strike and missile defense in the 1970s and 1980s. These high-tech capabilities likely helped deter Soviet aggression by asserting U.S. and NATO [North Atlantic Treaty Organization] forces could attack Warsaw Pact troops, military and political leaders, or civilian populations in response. When the Cold War ended, they continued to give America a military advantage over less capable, internally-focused competitors such as Iraq, North Korea, Russia, and—for a time—China.

This is changing as America's rivals build up their militaries and turn outward in an effort to gain territory and influence or distract their populations from internal grievances. They are increasingly empowered in this effort by the flattening of the research and development landscape. During the Cold War, American government and private institutions created the majority of patents as well as unpatented military advancements. Today most new patents originate outside the United States and scientific journals regularly feature articles by Chinese and Russian researchers in areas such as underwater acoustics, electronics engineering, materials science, and computer processing.

Today the U.S. military again finds itself in a long-term competition and at a disadvantage geographically and numerically; this time against a more diverse set of adversaries than during the Cold War. In Europe, East Asia, and the Middle East U.S. forces are opposing efforts by state and non-state rivals to erode the sovereignty or stability of American allies and partners, aided by high-end technology that enables long-range surveillance and strike capabilities designed to thwart U.S. power projection. DOD plans to address this multifaceted challenge in part through a "Third Offset Strategy" that will leverage technological leaps in areas of current U.S. military advantage to impose costs on competitors and demonstrate the ability to hinder or defeat their aggression.

DOD intends its Third Offset Strategy to build on U.S. superiority in areas such as undersea warfare, long-range precision strike, air warfare, and battle networks and is implementing long range plans to guide its research. But unlike the previous Offset Strategies that focused on a small set of operational concepts and shifted significant funding to their supporting technologies, DOD's current plans appear to cover a wide range of technologies without operational concepts or significant resource reallocation. This lack of focus will significantly reduce the advantage the U.S. military can establish and delay relevant capabilities.

EXPLOITING EMERGING TECHNOLOGICAL SHIFTS

DOD needs a coherent and disciplined technology strategy instead of "watering all the flowers" with its current approach. The two most significant challenges this strategy should address are threats to America's ability to project power and paramilitary or insurgent threats to the sovereignty of its allies in Europe and Asia. It needs to address these challenges by establishing enduring advantages for U.S. forces, rather than just gaining the upper hand temporarily.

America created enduring advantages in previous competitions by anticipating and preparing for the next phase in important warfare areas. For example, early in the Cold War, the U.S. Navy realized nuclear submarines would introduce a new phase of undersea warfare dominated by passive sonar and submarine quieting. It expanded investment in these capabilities and dominated the undersea against the Soviets for decades. Similarly, the U.S. Air Force saw how stealth and passive sensing would dramatically change air warfare and aggressively developed these capabilities. They did not reach the force until the Cold War's end, but stealth technologies have given U.S. forces the unique ability to strike targets conventionally anywhere on the globe for the last 25 years.

America's adversaries are now quickly catching up in these and other missions. DOD needs to identify the next phases in warfare areas where DOD has an advantage today that it must protect to be able to credibly deter and defeat aggression in the future. These include:

Undersea Warfare: The U.S. military's ability to project power against high-end adversaries hinges on the ability of its undersea forces to circumvent enemy air and surface defenses. As quiet submarines become the norm and passive sonars reach their range and size limits, active sonar and non-acoustic submarine detection will come to dominate undersea warfare. This could also increase the risk to U.S. submarines near adversary shores and compel them to shift from being tactical platforms, like fighter aircraft, to being host and coordination platforms, like aircraft carriers. To maintain its undersea dominance in light of these two shifts, DOD should focus on concepts and technologies for:

- Low frequency active sonar: They have longer ranges than today's shipboard sonars, but with lower resolution. Improved processing power will continue improving the accuracy of these systems.
- Active sonar countermeasures: As with radar above the water, jammers and decoys will become essential to spoof, confuse, and defeat enemy active sonars.
- Unmanned undersea vehicles (UUV): Particularly small ones that are hard to detect and can be bought and deployed in large numbers and large ones that can act as "trucks" to deploy seabed payloads and UUVs in coastal waters.
- Seabed payloads: Long-endurance sensors, communication relays, and power supplies for UUVs will be a key component of future undersea networks that enable submarines and other forces to support and control UUVs while finding and engaging enemy undersea forces.

Strike Warfare: U.S. forces must be able to threaten targets an enemy values or may use to coerce U.S. allies. Passive and active measures including underground facilities and surface-to-air missiles are changing today's precision strike advantage into a strike vs. missile defense competition. DOD should pursue the following concepts and technologies to sustain its strike capability:

- Overwhelming defenses: Smaller, cheaper networked weapons are emerging that can be launched in large numbers. They will be able to find and classify targets in flight and collaborate to ensure intended targets are destroyed—even if some strike weapons are lost to enemy defenses on the way.
- Disrupting defenses: High-powered microwave (HPM) transmitters are becoming small enough to go on missiles and bombs, while becoming powerful and selectable enough to damage or disrupt enemy sensors, weapons, and control systems at standoff range.
- Reaching hardened and buried targets: New burrowing and electromagnetic pulse weapons offer the ability to reach locations enemies attempt to place out of reach without having to resort to unsustainably large salvos.

Air Warfare: U.S. forces have been able to establish air superiority at will since the end of the Cold War. But improving low-probability of detection (LPD) sensors and sophisticated long-range missiles are reducing the value of aircraft speed and maneuverability and favoring larger aircraft able to carry larger sensors and weapons payloads. To sustain its current air superiority, DOD should prioritize concepts and technologies for:

- Longer-range LPD classification sensors: Historically, air engagements are won by the first pilot to classify a contact as enemy and shoot. Emerging long and medium wave passive infrared sensors and laser detection and ranging systems will enable U.S. fighters and air defenses to detect and classify enemy aircraft farther away without themselves being classified.
- Smaller, less expensive missiles: New energetic materials are making motors and warheads smaller, while new materials and processors are shrinking guidance systems. The resulting weapons can be bought and carried in larger numbers.
- Directed energy: Solid state laser and HPM weapons are reaching maturity. They offer greater capacity for air defense than traditional interceptor systems such as Patriot and can be small enough to be carried on larger aircraft as an offensive or defensive system.

Electromagnetic (EM) Spectrum Operations: The continued sophistication of radar and radar detectors will drive EM operations toward stealth and passive or LPD sensors and communications. DOD should advance the following concepts and technologies to achieve an enduring advantage in its battle networks:

- Multi-spectral stealth: New aircraft and ships incorporate features to reduce their radar signature. Stealth must now reduce the detectability of platforms to IR, UV, or acoustic detection as well.
- Networked, agile multi-function EM operations: Active Electronically Scanned Arrays (AESA) in the RF spectrum and focal plane arrays in the IR spectrum are becoming cheaper and smaller and can simultaneously transmit and receive over a wide range of frequencies. They can be incorporated on almost every platform and vehicle to conduct sensing, communication, and counter-sensing operations, enabling new multi-platform passive and LPD sensing and communication concepts.

- "Intelligent" EM operations: DOD must go beyond automating radio, jammer, or radar operations and instead get inside the enemy's decision loop. Emerging technologies can sense the EM environment, identify both known and unfamiliar threats, and manage EM operations to conduct friendly operations while denying those of the enemy. Intelligent EM systems being developed today will enable U.S. forces to get inside the enemy's decision loop and dominate the EM spectrum.

THE IMPORTANCE OF OPERATIONAL CONCEPTS

New technologies will not establish an enduring advantage for U.S. forces unless they are employed in operational concepts that achieve friendly objectives while denying those of the enemy. For example, stealth without a concept for how it could be used to conduct precision strike or air interdiction would not be a game-changing technology. Similarly, passive sonar without concepts for using it to track and threaten enemy submarines would not yield an operational benefit.

One effective approach for identifying promising combinations of concept and technology is wargaming, which Deputy Secretary Work has reinvigorated in the DOD. These games, however, have not yet translated into new operational concepts that guide technology investments, acquisition requirements, or resource allocation. Unless the insights from them are analyzed further and acted upon, DOD will continue to pursue new versions of today's capabilities. This approach may yield, at best, temporary advantages.

REFORMING HOW WE FIELD TECHNOLOGY

Acquisition reform must be an element of any attempt to innovate within DOD. Specifically, reform is needed to address unnecessarily high costs for new weapons systems that threaten to crowd out other new capabilities and protracted development timelines that prevent new technologies from getting to warfighters in time for them to be relevant.

Acquisition reform initiatives being pursued by DOD and Congress focus on improving accountability, but the most significant hindrance to developing affordable systems on time and budget is the requirements process. By defining requirements for new acquisition programs in isolation from technical or fiscal considerations, DOD makes it more likely new systems will use immature technologies while costing more and taking longer than expected. Further, rather than defining requirements and then allowing the acquisition system to develop a range of solutions to different elements of those requirements, DOD currently writes a set of requirements tailored to each new system, essentially eliminating the competition of ideas that might otherwise ensue.

Some improvements are being implemented today to bring acquisition and technology concerns into requirements development, but these are personality and system dependent. Instead, DOD should expand the development of new systems to meet already-existing requirements through prototyping and demonstration programs. This approach is already being used by organizations such as the OSD [Office of the Secretary of Defense] Strategic Capabilities Office (SCO) and Air Force Rapid Capabilities Office (RCO). It enables new systems to emerge from combinations of new operational concepts and technologies grounded in what is achievable and feasible in the near-term, rather than a "wish list" of what a new weapons system would ideally do in 20 years (when it would otherwise be fielded). In this approach requirements are used to evaluate the proposed system, rather than driving its development from the start.

These efforts should be expanded in DOD and used as the basis for reforming the requirements process, particularly for smaller systems. Platforms such as ships and aircraft have long lifetimes and are designed to carry and support warfighters; a more deliberate requirements process would be appropriate for them. Payloads such as missiles and sensors generally have shorter lifetimes and faster technology refresh cycles. Their requirements may be defined less explicitly in advance and could be developed or evaluated in conjunction with prototype and demonstration efforts that evaluate their feasibility.

CONCLUSION

The U.S. military has enjoyed unrivaled superiority since the end of the Cold War, but the technological and operational advantages it has relied upon are quickly eroding in the face of proliferating weapons and widely available commercial technology. DOD and civilian research and analysis efforts offer the potential to sustain and enhance DOD's advantages in support of a Third Offset Strategy. In its implementation, however, the DOD's current initiatives perpetuate today's diffused and unfocused efforts to develop new capabilities. Unless it changes, the result will be a shrinking number of expensive weapons using Cold War-era technology, a decline in American influence, and allies unsure of America's ability to protect their interests.

About the Center for Strategic and Budgetary Assessments
The Center for Strategic and Budgetary Assessments (CSBA)is an independent, nonpartisan policy research institute established to promote innovative thinking and debate about national security strategy and investment options. CSBA's analysis focuses on key questions related to existing and emerging threats to U.S. national security, and its goal is to enable policymakers to make informed decisions on matters of strategy, security policy, and resource allocation.

Chairman MCCAIN. Thank you.
Mr. Scharre?

STATEMENT OF PAUL SCHARRE, SENIOR FELLOW AND DIRECTOR OF THE 20YY WARFARE INITIATIVE, THE CENTER FOR A NEW AMERICAN SECURITY

Mr. SCHARRE. Thank you, Chairman McCain, Ranking Member Reed, distinguished Senators. It is an honor to be here today.

We are living in the midst today of an information revolution that is sweeping in its scope and scale. There is about $3.8 trillion spent every year on information technology, and that is more than double all military spending, R&D [Research and Development] procurement personnel by every country on earth combined.

Now, that is maturing a number of underlying technologies and sensors, computer processing, data networking that will have significant impacts on how militaries fight. It is already having those impacts today.

So we are seeing changes in warfare much like how the industrial revolution led to changes in World War I and World War II in tanks and aircraft and submarines. The U.S. has already been able to be a first mover in the information revolution and gain many of the fruits of this technology with things like GPS [global positioning systems] and stealth and things others have mentioned today.

Now, the challenge that we have is this technology is proliferating to others. We got an early move, but we do not get a monopoly. As Chairman McCain mentioned, many of those investments are happening outside of the defense sector.

So we saw in the Gulf War what some of these technologies can do in terms of inflicting significant damage and lethality on the enemy. But now we are going to have to face that same technology in warfare.

There is precedent for these kinds of changes. In the late 19th century, the British developed an early model machine gun, a Maxim gun, that they used for conquests all across Africa. But in World War I, they faced an enemy that also had machine guns with incredible devastating effects. In the Battle of the Somme, the British lost 20,000 men in a single day.

We are not prepared for those changes that are coming as this technology proliferates to others and then continues to evolve and mature.

Thousands of anti-tank guided missiles now litter the Middle East and North Africa in the hands of non-state groups. Countries like China and Russia are developing increasingly capable electronic warfare and long-range precision strike weapons and anti-space capabilities, all of which threaten our traditional modes of power projection.

Now that they have guided weapons, they can target our forces with great precision as well, saturating and overwhelming our defenses. Now, today missile defenses are very costly and the cost-exchange ratio favors the offense.

Now, this vulnerability of our major power projection assets, our carriers, our ships, tanks, our bases, coincides with the very unfortunate long-term trend in U.S. defense spending in decreasing numbers of capital assets. This precedes the current budget problem and will continue beyond it unless there are some major changes.

For several decades, the per-unit cost of our ships and aircraft has steadily risen, shrinking the number of assets that we can afford. Now, to date our response is to build more capable assets. We have extremely capable, qualitatively capable, ships and aircraft and submarines and aircraft carriers. But, of course, this drives costs up even further, reducing our quantities even more.

Now, this has made sense in a world where others do not have weapons that can target us with great precision. We have been willing to make this trade, and we have done so in many cases very deliberately trading quantity for quality.

But this is no longer going to work in a world where others can target us as well with great precision; can concentrate their fire power on our shrinking number of major combat assets. We are putting more and more eggs into a smaller number of vulnerable baskets.

Now, the Department of Defense broadly refers to these challenges as anti-access/area denial. The problem is reasonably well understood. The problem is in launching a new offset strategy to counter it. A better ship or better aircraft alone is not going to solve the problem because on the path we have been on with the acquisition system and our requirements system that we have, we will build something that is even more expensive that will be good but even more expensive, and we will have even fewer of them.

So to operate in this area, we need a more fundamental shift in our military thinking. We need to be able to disperse our forces, disaggregate our capabilities into larger numbers of lower cost systems, operate and deceive the enemy through deception measures and decoys, and we need to be able to swarm and overwhelm enemy defenses with large numbers of low cost assets.

Now, so early thinking along these lines is underway in many parts of the Department. The Army's new operating concept talks about dispersed operations inside anti-access areas. The Marine Corps is also experimenting with distributed operations inside the littorals. The Naval Postgraduate School is researching aerial swarm combat with a 50-on-50 dog fight between swarm drones that they are working to develop. DARPA's [Defence Advanced Research Projects Agency] System of Systems Integration Technology and Experimentation program—it is one of those long DOD acronyms called SoSITE, S-o-S-I-T-E—aims to disaggregate aircraft capabilities entirely into a swarm of low cost expendable, cooperative assets.

So collectively these hint at the next paradigm shift in warfare, from fighting as a network of a very small number of expensive, exclusive assets as we do today to fighting as a swarm of a large number of cooperative distributed assets.

The main obstacles that stand in our way are not fundamentally technological. We could build the technology and within a reasonable defense budget if we are willing to make trades. They are not financial. The main obstacle is conceptual. It is a willingness to experiment with new ways of warfighting, and it is urgent that we begin this process of experimentation now.

Thank you very much.

[The prepared statement of Mr. Scharre follows:]

PREPARED STATEMENT BY PAUL SCHARRE

DISRUPTIVE CHANGE IN WARFARE

Warfare—the way in which militaries fight—is constantly evolving. Militaries compete in a cycle of innovations, countermeasures, and counter-countermeasures in an attempt to gain an advantage over their enemies. War is a punishing environment, and even a small edge in capability can lead to dramatically different outcomes. A slightly longer-range sensor, missile, or longer spear can mean the difference between life and death. Occasionally, some innovations lead to a major disruption in warfare that changes the rules of the game entirely. Better horse cavalry no longer matter when the enemy has tanks. Better battleships are irrelevant in an age of aircraft carriers. New technologies are often catalysts for these changes, but it is their combination with doctrinal and organizational innovations in war that leads to paradigm shifts on the battlefield. Tanks or aircraft alone might be beneficial, but they require new training, organizations, and concepts for use to create the *blitzkrieg*.

Even while militaries seek ordinary, incremental gains over adversaries, they must constantly be on guard for disruptive changes that revolutionize warfare. This challenge is particularly acute for dominant military powers, such as the United States today, who are heavily invested in existing ways of fighting while underdogs must innovate by necessity.

Are we on the verge of another paradigm shift in warfare? On what timeframe? Is one already underway? If so, what early conclusions can we draw about these changes? There are two elements driving changes in warfare that will unfold in the coming decades:

The first is the proliferation of existing advanced technologies to a wider range of actors. Even though these technologies already exist, their proliferation to multiple actors across the international system will change the operating environment for U.S. forces. Technologies that the United States has itself used in war, but not yet faced on the battlefield, are finding their way into the hands of potential adversaries. This will force changes in U.S. concepts of operation and capabilities, changes that can be seen in nascent form today but have not yet fully matured.

Technology does not stand still, however. The information revolution, which has already yielded advances such as GPS, stealth, and precision-guided weapons, continues apace. Advances in autonomy, cyber weapons, data fusion, electronic warfare, synthetic biology, and other areas are likely to drive significant changes in military capabilities. This second driving force—the continued maturation of the information revolution—could lead to even more profound changes in how militaries fight.

The U.S. military must prepare for these changes to come, which will inevitably unfold at uneven rates and in surprising ways. While no one can predict the future, U.S. defense spending represents a *de facto* prediction about what sorts of capabilities planners believe are likely to be useful in future conflicts. Research and development (R&D) and procurement investments often take decades to mature and yield platforms that stay in the force for even longer. The new Air Force long range strike bomber (LRS–B) will not reach initial operational capability for 10 years and will likely remain in the force for decades beyond. The B–52 bomber has been in service for 60 years. This year, the U.S. Navy began laying the keel for a new aircraft carrier, the *USS John F. Kennedy* (CVN–79), which will remain in active service until 2070. These investments represent multi-billion dollar bets that warfare will evolve in such a way that these capabilities will remain useful for decades to come.

Disruptive change is a near certainty over these timescales, however. The twentieth century saw major disruptive changes in warfare in World War I, World War II, the Cold War with the advent of nuclear weapons, and the Gulf War with first-generation information age weapons such as stealth, GPS, and precision strike. Thus, it is imperative that military planners peer as best they can into an uncertain future to try to understand the shape of changes to come.

THE FUTURE IS ALREADY HERE

Science fiction author William Gibson, who coined the term *cyberspace,* has remarked, "The future is already here, it's just not evenly distributed yet." Many of the changes to come in warfare will come not from new technologies, but from the diffusion of existing ones throughout the international system.[1] The resulting difference in scale of a technology's use can often lead to dramatically different effects. A single car can help a person get from point A to point B faster. A world full of cars is one with superhighways, gridlock, smog, suburbia, road rage, and climate change. In war, the battlefield environment can look dramatically different when one technology proliferates to many actors.

There is historical precedent for such changes. At the end of the nineteenth century, the British used an early model machine gun, the Maxim Gun, to aid their conquests of Africa. This technology gave them a decisive advantage over indigenous forces who did not have it. Machine gun technology rapidly proliferated to European competitors, however, resulting in a very different battlefield environment. In World War I, the British faced an enemy who also had machine guns and the result was disaster. At the Battle of the Somme, Britain lost 20,000 men killed in a single day. Their concepts for warfighting had failed to evolve to their new reality.

Today the United States faces a similar challenge. The 1991 Gulf War hinted at the potential of information age warfare. U.S. battle networks comprised of sensors, communication links, and precision-guided weapons allowed U.S. forces to employ great lethality on the battlefield against Iraqi forces.[2] The United States had these advantages because it was a first-mover in the information revolution, capitalizing on these opportunities before others.[3]

Now these same technologies are proliferating to others and the result is a very different operating environment. Thousands of anti-tank guided missiles are in the hands of non-state groups in the Middle East and North Africa. Countries such as China are building long-range missiles to target our bases and ships. Now that others have guided weapons, they can target U.S. forces with great precision, saturating and overwhelming U.S. defenses. Missile interceptors to defend our assets are costly, and the cost-exchange ratios favor the offense.

This vulnerability of major U.S.—power projection platforms—our ships, air bases, and aircraft—to precision-guided weapons is particularly unfortunate because it coincides with a long-term trend in decreasing numbers of U.S. major combat systems. For several decades, per unit costs for ships and aircraft have steadily risen, shrinking the number of major combat assets the United States can afford. This trend preceded the current budget crunch and, unless corrected, will continue long after.

To date, the U.S. response has been to make its platforms more capable to offset their reduced numbers. This has further driven up costs, exacerbating this trend. In a world where the enemy has unguided weapons, the United States has been willing to accept this trade. The U.S. has fewer ships and aircraft in its inventory than twenty years ago, but they are more capable.

But in a world where the enemy can target U.S. forces with a high-degree of precision, having a small number of exquisite systems creates an enormous vulnerability, because the enemy has fewer targets on which to concentrate firepower.

The Department of Defense broadly refers to these adversary capabilities as "anti-access / area denial" (A2/AD), because any U.S. forces within their range will be vulnerable to attack.[4] The Department of Defense has launched a new offset strategy to regain American military technical superiority. But the solution to this problem cannot be merely a better ship or aircraft. On the current trajectory, those assets

---

[1] Michael Horowitz, *The Diffusion of Military Power: Causes and Consequences for International Politics* (New Jersey: Princeton)

[2] Max Boot, *War Made New: Weapons, Warriors, and the Making of the Modern World* (Gotham, 2006).

[3] Barry Watts, *The Evolution of Precision Strike* (Washington DC: Center for Strategic and Budgetary Assessments, 2013).

[4] U.S. Department of Defense, *Air-Sea Battle: Service Collaboration to Address Anti-Access & Area Denial Challenges* (Washington DC, 2013).

would be even more expensive and purchased in fewer numbers, placing even more eggs in a smaller number of vulnerable baskets.

A more fundamental shift in American military thinking is needed. To operate against adversaries with precision-guided weapons, the U.S. needs to disperse its forces, disaggregate its capabilities, confuse enemy sensors through decoys and deception, and swarm enemy defenses with large numbers of expendable assets.

Early thinking along these lines is already underway in many corners of the Department of Defense. The Army's new operating concept includes dispersed operations for anti-access environments.[5] The Marine Corps is experimenting with distributed operations across the littorals. The Naval Postgraduate School is researching aerial swarm combat.[6] DARPA's System of Systems Integration Technology and Experimentation program aims to disaggregate aircraft capabilities into a swarm of cooperative, low cost expendable air vehicles.[7]

Collectively, these efforts hint at the next paradigm shift in warfare: from fighting as a network of a few, expensive platforms as we do today; to in the future fighting as a swarm of many, low cost assets that can coordinate their actions to achieve a collective whole. The diffusion of advanced military technology is also increasing the number of actors who can effectively contest U.S. forces in certain domains—undersea, the electromagnetic spectrum, space, and cyberspace. Areas where the United States has largely had freedom of maneuver to date are now becoming increasingly congested, requiring new U.S. responses.

As the U.S. military adjusts to a world of proliferated precision-guided weapons and adapts its concepts of operation to counter-A2/AD capabilities, it must also be cognizant of even more dramatic changes to come.

THE UNFOLDING INFORMATION REVOLUTION

The information revolution has already led to significant changes in warfare by enabling the advanced sensors, communications networks, and guided weapons that led to U.S. superiority and now anti-access capabilities as they proliferate. But the information revolution is not stopping. $3.8 trillion is invested annually in information technology, roughly double all military spending—procurement, R&D, personnel, construction—of every country on earth.[8] While the United States was an early first-mover in information technology, the fruits of the massive commercial sector investments in better sensors, processors, and networks will be available to many.

The scale of this investment, along with the continued exponential growth in computing power, virtually guarantees disruptive change.[9] But in what ways will the continuing information revolution change warfare? Specific military applications may not yet be known, but we can look at underlying trends in what information technology enables. Across the many diverse applications of information technology run three core trends: increasing transparency, connectivity, and machine intelligence.

Increasing transparency

One of the core features of the information revolution is the "datafication" of our world—the generation of large amounts of digital data. Combined with the fact that computers make it virtually costless to copy information, this has resulted in a freer flow of information that is making the world increasingly transparent. Satellite images, once the province only of superpowers, are now available free online. Police and security services have found their activities subject to unprecedented scrutiny and are scrambling to adapt, even in the United States.[10] Even secret government

[5] U.S. Army, *The U.S. Army Operating Concept: Win in a Complex World, 2020–2040,* October 31, 2014, *http://www.tradoc.army.mil/tpubs/pams/tp525-3-1.pdf.*

[6] Rollin Bishop, "Record-Breaking Drone Swarm Sees 50 UAVs Controlled by a Single Person," *Popular Mechanics,* September 16, 2015, *http://www.popularmechanics.com/flight/drones/news/a17371/record-breaking-drone-swarm/.*

[7] Defense Advanced Research Projects Agency, "System of Systems Integration Technology and Experimentation (SoSITE)," *http://www.darpa.mil/program/system-of-systems-integration-technology-and-experimentation.*

[8] "Gartner Says Worldwide IT Spending to Grow 2.4 percent in 2015," *Gartner.com,* January 12, 2015, *http://www.gartner.com/newsroom/id/2959717.*

[9] Computing power continues advancing at an exponential rate, but the pace of change has begun to decline. See "Performance Development," *Top500.org, http://www.top500.org/statistics/perfdevel/;* and Michael Feldman, "Life Beyond Moore's Law," *Top500.org, http://www.top500.org/blog/life-beyond-moores-law/.*

[10] Scott Calvert, "In Baltimore, Arrests Down and Crime Up," *Wall Street Journal,* May 20, 2015, *http://www.wsj.com/articles/in-baltimore-arrests-down-and-crime-up-1432162121.* Mi-

Continued

data is not as secret as it once was. According to the U.S. government, Edward Snowden stole in excess of an estimated 1.7 million documents, the largest leak in history.[11] A leak of such scale would have been nearly impossible in a pre-digital era. The Vietnam Era Pentagon Papers, by comparison, were a mere 7,000 pages photocopied by hand.[12] The datafication of our world combined with the ease with which digital information can be copied and shared is leading to a world that is more transparent, with secrets harder to keep on all sides. Sifting through this massive amount of data, particularly when it is unstructured and heterogeneous, becomes a major challenge.

Increasing connectivity

Information technology is increasing the degree of connectivity between people and things, both in terms of the number of people and things online as well as the volume and bandwidth of information exchanged. As the Internet continues to colonize the material world, more objects are increasingly networked (e.g., Internet of things), enabling remote access and information-sharing, as well as making them susceptible to hacking. Social media enables many-to-many communication, allowing any individual to share their story or report on abuses of authorities. The result is a fundamental shift in communication power dynamics, upending relationships between individuals and traditional authorities. In addition, connectivity allows crowdsourcing of problems and ideas, accelerating the pace of innovation and the momentum of human communication.

Increasingly intelligent machines

The rapid growth in computing power is resulting in increasingly intelligent machines. When embodied in physical machines, this trend is allowing the growth of increasingly capable and autonomous munitions and robotic systems.[13] Advanced computing also allows for the processing of large amounts of data, including gene sequencing, enabling advances in "big data," artificial intelligence, and synthetic biology. While current computing methods have limitations and face tapering growth rates, possible novel computing methods, such as quantum computing or neural networks, hold potential for continued growth in intelligent machines.[14]

SIX CONTESTS THAT WILL SHAPE THE FUTURE OF WARFARE

As militaries weigh how to spend scarce defense dollars, they must grapple with the challenge of predicting which attributes will be most valuable in the decades to come. Should they focus on speed, stealth, range, sensing, data processing, armor, mobility, or other areas? All of these attributes are valuable, but which will be most crucial to surviving the conflicts of the 21st Century?

As the information revolution continues to mature, six key operational concepts will shape the future of warfare:

1. Hiding vs. Finding
2. Understanding vs. Confusion
3. Network Resilience vs. Network Degradation
4. Hitting vs. Intercepting
5. Speed of Action vs. Speed of Decision-Making
6. Shaping the Perceptions of Key Populations

These contests are a product of both the proliferation of existing guided weapons, sensors, and networks as well as future advancements in information technology. Militaries will seek to both exploit these technologies for their own gain, finding enemies on the battlefield and striking them with great precision, as well as develop countermeasures to conceal their forces, sow confusion among the enemy, degrade enemy networks, and intercept incoming projectiles. As they do so, information-based technologies will not be the only ones that will be useful. Advances in directed

---

chael S. Schmidt and Matt Apuzzo, "F.B.I. Chief Links Scrutiny of Police With Rise in Violent Crime," *New York Times,* October 23, 2015, *http://www.nytimes.com/2015/10/24/us/politics/ fbi-chief-links-scrutiny-of-police-with-rise-in-violent-crime.html?_r=0.*

[11] Chris Strohm and Del Quentin Wilber, "Pentagon says Snowden took most U.S. secrets ever: Rogers," *Bloomberg,com,* January 9, 2014, *http://www.bloomberg.com/news/articles/ 2014–01–09/pentagon-finds-snowden-took-1-7-million-filesrogers-says.*

[12] Douglas O. Linder, "The Pentagon Papers (Daniel Ellsberg) Trial: An Account," 2011, *http://law2.umkc.edu/faculty/projects/ftrials/ellsberg/ellsbergaccount.html.*

[13] Robert Work and Shawn Brimley, *20YY: Preparing for War in the Robotic Age* (Washington DC: Center for a New American Security, 2014). Paul Scharre, *Robotics on the Battlefield Part 1: Range, Persistence and Daring* (Washington DC: CNAS, 2014), and *Robotics on the Battlefield Part 2: The Coming Swarm* (Washington DC: CNAS 2015. From a certain perspective, a guided weapon is a simple robot.

[14] *Top500.org.*

energy weapons or electromagnetic rail guns to intercept enemy guided weapons, for example, have great potential value. But the scale of changes in greater transparency, connectivity, and more intelligent machines will make capitalizing on these advantages and countering adversaries' attempts to do so critical for gaining an operational advantage in the battlefields of the twenty-first century. While militaries will seek dominance on both sides of these contests, technological developments may tilt the balance to favor one or the other side over time.

Hiding vs. Finding

One of the prominent features of information-enabled warfare to-date is the development of precision-guided weapons that can strike ships, aircraft, and bases at long distances. Defensively, this has placed a premium on hiding. Non-state groups seek to blend into civilian populations. State actors increasingly rely on mobile systems, such as mobile air defense systems and mobile missile launchers. Because of these innovations in hiding, offensive operations are often limited by intelligence, surveillance, and reconnaissance (ISR) capabilities. For the past two decades, the United States has been on the offensive side of this exchange. However, adversary developments in long-range precision strike are forcing the United States to think more carefully about concealment strategies as well. Because precision-guided weapons can deliver a high volume of lethal firepower directly on a target, whoever gets the first salvo may decide victory. Getting that first shot may also depend increasingly on one's ability to effectively hide, while deploying sufficient sensors to find the enemy first. The maxim "look first, shoot first, kill first" may apply not only in beyond visual range air-to-air combat, but in all domains of warfare.

One important asymmetry in the hiding vs. finding contest is the ability to leverage increasing computer processing power to sift through noise to detect objects, including synthesizing information gained from multiple active or passive sensors. This makes it increasingly difficult for those seeking to hide because they must conceal their signature or actively deceive the enemy in multiple directions at once and potentially against multiple methods of detection. Advanced electronic warfare measures enable precision jamming and deception, but these methods require knowing the location of enemy sensors, which may be passive.[15] Thus, a contest of hiding and finding capital assets may first depend on a preliminary contest of hiding and finding distributed sensors and jammers lurking in the battlespace. These techniques, both for distributed passive sensing and distributed precision electronic warfare, depend upon effectively networked, cooperative forces, which are intimately linked with other contests.[16]

Certain domains of warfare may have inherent characteristics that make hiding more or less difficult, changing where militaries make their investments over time. Warfare undersea is likely to become increasingly important, as the underwater environment offers a relative sanctuary from which militaries can project power well inside adversaries' anti-access zones. Cross-domain capabilities that allow militaries to project power from the undersea into air and land may be increasingly useful. Conversely, as other nations develop counter-space capabilities, U.S. investments in space are increasingly at risk. During the Cold War, the U.S. and U.S.S.R. had a tacit understanding that counter-space capabilities were destabilizing, since they could be seen as a prelude to a nuclear first strike. However, the era of U.S. sanctuary in space is over as U.S. satellites face an increasing array of threats from kinetic and non-kinetic weapons as well as the specter of cascading space debris.[17] Satellites move through predictable orbits in space and maneuvering expends precious fuel, making them inherently vulnerable to attack. This vulnerability places a premium on redundant non-space backups to enhance U.S. resiliency and diminish the incentives for an adversary to strike first in space.

Technology areas that could enhance hiding or finding include:

- Hiding
  o Adaptive and responsive jamming
  o Precision electronic attack
  o Counter-space capabilities (kinetic and non-kinetic)

---

[15] Mark J. Mears, "Cooperative Electronic Attack Using Unmanned Air Vehicles," Air Force Research Lab, Wright-Patterson Air Force Base, *http://www.dtic.mil/dtic/tr/fulltext/u2/a444985.pdf.*

[16] Paul Scharre, "Robotics on the Battlefield Part II: The Coming Swarm," 32.

[17] Brian Weeden, "The End of Sanctuary in Space," *War is Boring, https://medium.com/war-is-boring/the-end-of-sanctuary-in-space-2d58fba741a#.u6i8y2rpd.* On the prospect of a runaway cascade of space debris, see Donald J. Kessler and Burton G. Cour-Palais (1978). "Collision Frequency of Artificial Satellites: The Creation of a Debris Belt". *Journal of Geophysical Research* **83**: 2637–2646, *http://onlinelibrary.wiley.com/doi/10.1029/JA083iA06p02637/abstract.*

o Metamaterials for electromagnetic and auditory cloaking
o Cyber defenses
o Low-cost autonomous decoys
o Undersea capabilities—submarines, autonomous uninhabited undersea vehicles, and undersea payload modules
o Quantum encryption techniques (which can sense if the communications link is being intercepted)[18]
- Finding
o Sensor fusion / data fusion
o Distributed sensing
o Foliage-penetrating radar
o Resilient space-based surveillance
o Low-signature uninhabited vehicles for surveillance
o Low-cost robotic systems, including leveraging commercial components for clandestine surveillance
o Long-endurance power solutions (such as radioisotope power) to enable persistent robotic surveillance systems
o Networked, undersea sensors
o Cyber espionage
o Quantum computing (to break encryption)[19]

Understanding vs. Confusion

As the volume and pace of information on the battlefield increases (including misinformation), turning information into *understanding* will be key. A key contest in war will be between adversary cognitive systems, both artificial and human, to process information, understand the battlespace, and decide and execute faster than the enemy. Advances in machine intelligence show great promise for increasing the ability of artificial cognitive systems to understand and react to information in intelligent, goal-oriented ways. However, machine intelligence remains "brittle." While it is possible to design machines that can outperform humans in narrow tasks, such as driving, chess, or answering trivia, human intelligence far outstrips machines in terms of its robustness and adaptability to a wide range of problems. For the foreseeable future, the best cognitive systems are likely to be hybrid architectures combining human and machine cognition, leveraging the advantages of each.[20]

These technologies also offer the potential for new vulnerabilities, as militaries will attempt to thwart their enemies' ability to understand the operating environment by denying accurate information, planting misinformation, and sowing doubt in whatever information an enemy already has. Deception has been a key component of military operations for millennia and will remain so in the future, and these technologies will offer new opportunities for increasing confusion.[21]

Technology areas that could affect understanding or confusion include:

- Understanding
o Artificial cognitive systems
  - Advanced microprocessor design[22]
  - Data processing and "big data" analytics
  - Artificial intelligence, neural networks, and "deep learning"
- Human cognitive performance enhancement
  - Pharmaceutical enhancements, such as Adderall or Modafinil
  - Training methods, such as transcranial direct current stimulation
  - Synthetic biology
- Human-machine synthesis
  - Human factors engineering and human-machine interfaces
  - Brain-computer interfaces[23]

---

[18] This technique is called quantum key distribution. For an overview, see Valerio Scarani et al., "The Security of Practical Quantum Key Distribution," Reviews of Modern Physics **81**, 1301, September 30, 2009, *http://arxiv.org/pdf/0802.4155.pdf*.

[19] Steven Rich and Barton Gellman, "NSA seeks to build quantum computer that could crack most types of encryption," *Washington Post*, January 2, 2014.

[20] Paul Scharre, "Centaur Warfighting: The False Choice of Humans vs. Automation" (forthcoming). Tyler Cowen, "What are Humans Still Good for? The Turning Point in Freestyle Chess may be Approaching," Marginal Revolution, November 5, 2013.

[21] For example, Sun Tzu wrote: "All warfare is based on deception." Sun Tzu, *The Art of War*, Chapter 1.

[22] *Top500.org*.

[23] For example, see Nick Stockton, "Woman Controls a Fighter Jet Sim Using Only Her Mind," *Wired*, March 5, 2015, *http://www.wired.com/2015/03/woman-controls-fighter-jet-sim-using-mind/*.

- • Synthetic telepathy
- Confusion
  - o Cyber espionage and sabotage
  - o Misinformation, deception, and spoofing attacks
  - o Human performance degradation
  - o Tailored biological weapons

An important asymmetry between the United States and potential adversaries is the uneasiness with which human enhancement technologies are viewed in the United States. While there are no legal or ethical objections *per se* to human enhancement, they raise many legal and ethical issues that must be addressed. Experiments with cognitively enhancing drugs and training techniques can and have been performed in military labs, meeting stringent legal and ethical requirements.[24] However, there remains a cultural prejudice in some military communities against human enhancement, even for treatments that have been shown to be both safe and effective. The Department of Defense currently lacks overarching policy guidance to the military services to articulate a path forward on human performance enhancing technologies.[25]

Network Resilience vs. Network Degradation

Networking allows military forces to fight as a coherent whole, rather than as individual, non-cohesive units. For the past two decades, the U.S. military has been able to leverage the advantages of a networked force and has largely fought with freedom of maneuver in space and the electromagnetic spectrum. However, military networks will be increasingly contested by jamming, cyber attacks, and physical attacks on communications nodes. Resilient networks that are flexible and adaptable in the face of attacks, as well as doctrine that can adapt to degraded network operations, will be key to maintaining a force that can fight through network attacks. This includes "thin line" redundant backups that may offer limited communications among distributed forces, as well as off-network solutions. While many solutions for network resilience encompass doctrine and training to fight under degraded network conditions, technological solutions are also important to maintain networks under stress. This includes not only communications, but also position, navigation, and timing data, which are critical for synchronized and precise global military operations.

Technology areas affecting network resilience and degradation include:

- • Network resilience
  - o Protected communications, such as low probability of intercept and detection communications
  - o High-altitude long-endurance aircraft or airships to function as pseudo-satellites ("pseudo-lites")
  - o Software-defined radios (to allow adaptable communications)
  - o Open-architecture communications systems, to allow rapid adaptability of hardware and software to respond to enemy jamming
  - o Cyber defenses
  - o Autonomous undersea vehicles (to protect undersea communications infrastructure)
  - o Lower-cost space launch options
  - o Faster-responsive space launch options to replenish degraded space architectures
  - o GPS-independent position, navigation, and timing
- • Network degradation
  - o Improved jamming techniques
  - o Offensive cyber weapons
  - o Anti-satellite weapons (kinetic and non-kinetic)
  - o High-powered microwave weapons to disrupt or destroy electronic systems

Hitting vs. Intercepting

Finding the enemy, understanding the data, and passing it to the right warfighting elements is only a prerequisite to achieving effects on target, frequently from missiles or torpedoes. If "knowing is half the battle," the other half is violence.

---

[24] For example, see Caldwell et al., "Modafinil's Effects on Simulator Performance and Mood on Pilots During 37 H Without Sleep," *Aviation, Space, and Environmental Medicine* (September 2004), 777–784, *http://www.ncbi.nlm.nih.gov/pubmed/15460629;* McKinley *et al.,* "Acceleration of Image Analyst Training with Transcranial Direct Current Stimulation," *Behavioral Neuroscience* (February 2015), *http://www.ncbi.nlm.nih.gov/pubmed/24341718.*

[25] For an overview, see Patrick Lin et al., "Enhanced Warfighters: Risk, Ethics, and Policy," January 1, 2013, *http://ethics.calpoly.edu/greenwall__report.pdf.*

Because guided weapons can put lethal effects directly on a target, intercepting inbound threats or diverting them with decoys is generally a more effective response than attempting to mitigate direct hits via improved armor. However, missile defense is a challenging task. Missiles are difficult to strike mid-flight, requiring multiple interceptors, resulting in cost-exchange ratios that currently favor the offense.

A number of possible technology breakthroughs could tilt this balance in either direction:

- Hitting
  o Networked, cooperative munitions, including cooperative decoys and jammers
  o Hypersonic weapons
  o Advanced stealth, both for missiles and aircraft
  o Large numbers of low-cost swarming missiles or uninhabited systems to saturate enemy defenses
  o Airborne, undersea, or sea surface arsenal ships or "missile trucks" to more cost-effectively transport missiles to the fight
  o High-fidelity decoys to increase the costs to defenders
  o Long-endurance uninhabited aircraft to enable long-range persistence and strike
- Intercepting
  o Low cost-per-shot electric weapons, such as high-energy lasers and electromagnetic rail guns
  o High quality radars for tracking incoming rounds and guiding interceptors
  o Long-endurance uninhabited aircraft for forward ballistic missile defense, both for launch detection and boost phase intercept
  o Persistent clandestine surveillance, from space assets, stealthy uninhabited aircraft, or unattended ground sensors for early detection of ballistic missile launch and pre-launch preparation

The U.S. military has long sought low cost-per-shot weapons such as high-energy lasers and electromagnetic rail guns to upend the missile defense cost-exchange ratio. High-energy lasers have already been demonstrated against slow-moving, unhardened targets such as low-cost drones or mortars. Current operationally-ready lasers are in the tens of kilowatts, however, and scaling up to sufficient power to intercept ballistic missiles would require on the order of a megawatt, more than an order of magnitude improvement.[26] While such improvements are frequently seen in computer-based technologies, laser technology and perhaps more importantly key enablers such as cooling and energy storage are not improving at such a rapid pace. Electromagnetic rail guns, on the other hand, currently show the most promise for defense against ballistic missiles. They require significant amounts of power, however, on the order of tens of megajoules, necessitating more advanced power management systems, similar to those on the DDG–1000 destroyer.[27]

Speed of Action vs. Speed of Decision-Making

Speed has always been a critical aspect of warfare. Understanding the battlefield and reacting faster than the enemy can help in achieving a decisive edge over one's adversary, forcing the enemy to confront a shifting, confusing chaotic landscape. In recent times, this has been instantiated in the American military concept of an "observe, orient, decide, act" (OODA) loop, where adversaries compete to complete this cycle faster than the enemy, thus changing the battle's conditions before the enemy can understand the situation and effectively respond. But the concept is ancient. Sun Tzu wrote, "Speed is the essence of war."[28]

Many emerging technologies have the potential to accelerate the pace of battle even further, including hypersonics, directed energy weapons, cyber weapons, and autonomous systems. Militaries will seek to leverage these technologies and other innovations, such as improved training, doctrine, or organizations, to understand and react faster than the enemy. Nascent developments in these areas highlight a different contest, however—the challenge commanders have in keeping control over their own forces on the battlefield.

[26] Jason Ellis, "Directed Energy Weapons: Promise and Prospects," *Center for a New American Security* (Washington, DC), April 2015, *http://www.cnas.org/sites/default/files/publications-pdf/CNAS_Directed_Energy_Weapons_April-2015.pdf.*

[27] Office of Naval Research, "Electromagnetic Railgun," *http://www.onr.navy.mil/Science-Technology/Departments/Code-35/All-Programs/air-warfare-352/Electromagnetic-Railgun.aspx;* U.S. Navy, "DDG–1000 fact sheet," *http://www.navsea.navy.mil/teamships/PEOS_DDG1000/DDG1000_factsheet.aspx.*

[28] Sun Tzu, *The Art of War,* Chapter 11. This statement is sometimes translated as "swiftness" or "rapidity" in place of "speed."

The tension between the speed of action on the battlefield and the speed of decision-making by commanders will be an important aspect of future warfare. Disaggregated and dispersed swarming tactics may be valuable for operating within A2/AD areas and decentralized control will push decision-making closer to the battlefield's edge, but this comes at a cost of less direct control for higher commanders. Coordinating action across a widely dispersed battlefield will improve operational effectiveness, but depends upon resilient networks and effective command and control architectures. Different militaries will balance these tensions in different ways, with some retaining centralized control and others delegating decision-making to battlefield commanders.

While this tension between centralized vs. decentralized command and control is not new, an important new dimension to this dilemma is the role of automation. Autonomous systems—robotics, data processing algorithms, and cyberspace tools—all have the potential to execute tasks far faster than humans. Automated stock trading, for example, happens at speeds measured in milliseconds.[29] Autonomous systems will pose advantages in reacting quickly to changing battlefield conditions. They also pose risks, however. Autonomous systems are "brittle"—if used outside of their intended operating conditions, they may fail unexpectedly and dramatically. Automated stock trading, for example, has played a role in "flash crashes," including the May 2010 flash crash where the U.S. stock market lost nearly 10 percent of its value in a matter of minutes.[30] Autonomous systems also may be more vulnerable to some forms of spoofing or behavioral hacking, which also allegedly played a role during the 2010 flash crash.[31] Militaries will therefore want to think hard about the balance of human and machine decision-making in their systems. "Human circuit breakers" may be valuable safeguards against hacking and failures in autonomous systems, even if they induce some delays.[32]

One example area where militaries already face this challenge is in defending against rocket, missile, and mortar attack. At least 30 countries have automated defensive systems to defend land bases, ships, and vehicles from saturation attacks that could overwhelm human operators.[33] These systems are vital for protecting military assets against salvos of guided munitions, but they are not without their drawbacks. In 2003, the U.S. Patriot air defense system shot down two friendly aircraft and its automation played a role in the incidents.[34]

Balancing the tension between the speed of action on the battlefield and the speed of decision-making by commanders is less about specific technologies than how those technologies are used and the training, rules of engagement, doctrine, and organizations that militaries employ. Realistic training under conditions of imperfect information and degraded networks can help prepare commanders for real-world situations that demand decisive, decentralized action. Improved human-machine interfaces and design can also help in retaining effective human control over high-speed

---

[29] Irene Aldridge, *High-Frequency Trading: A Practical Guide to Algorithmic Strategies and Trading Systems, 2nd Edition* (Wiley Trading, 2013), *http://www.amazon.com/gp/product/B00B0H9S5K/ref=dp-kindle-redirect?ie=UTF8&btkr=1.*

[30] U.S. Commodity Futures Trading Commission and U.S. Securities and Exchange Commission, *Findings Regarding the Market Events of May 6, 2010* (September 30, 2010), 2, *http://www.sec.gov/news/studies/2010/marketevents-report.pdf.* See also, Torben G. Andersen and Oleg Bondarenko, "VPIN and the Flash Crash," *Journal of Financial Markets* 17 (May 8, 2013), *http://papers.ssrn.com/sol3/papers.cfm?abstract_id=1881731*; David Easley, Marcos Lopez de Prado, and Maureen O'Hara, "The Microstructure of the 'Flash Crash': Flow Toxicity, Liquidity Crashes, and the Probability of Informed Trading," *The Journal of Portfolio Management,* 37, no. 2 (Winter 2011), *http://papers.ssrn.com/sol3/papers.cfm?abstract_id=1695041*; and Wes Bethel, David Leinweber, Oliver Ruebel, and Kesheng Wu, "Federal Market Information Technology in the Post Flash Crash Era: Roles for Supercomputing," *Proceedings of the Fourth Workshop on High Performance Computational Finance* (September 25, 2011), *http://papers.ssrn.com/sol3/papers.cfm?abstract_id=1939522.*

[31] Douwe Miedema and Sarah N. Lynch, "UK Speed Trader Arrested over Role in 2010 'Flash Crash'," *Reuters,* April 21, 2015, *http://www.reuters.com/article/2015/04/21/us-usa-security-fraud-idUSKBN0NC21220150421.*

[32] Paul Scharre and Michael C. Horowitz, "Keeping Killer Robots on a Tight Leash," *Defense One,* April 14, 2015, *http://www.defenseone.com/ideas/2015/04/keeping-killer-robots-tight-leash/110164/.*

[33] Paul Scharre and Michael C. Horowitz, "An Introduction to Autonomy in Weapon Systems," *Center for a New American Security,* February 2015, *http://www.cnas.org/sites/default/files/publications-pdf/Ethical%20Autonomy%20Working%20Paper_021015_v02.pdf.*

[34] John K. Hawley, "Looking Back at 20 Years of MANPRINT on Patriot: Observations and Lessons," *Army Research Laboratory,* September 2007, *http://www.arl.army.mil/arlreports/2007/ARL-SR-0158.pdf.* Office of the Under Secretary of Defense For Acquisition, Technology, and Logistics, *Report of the Defense Science Board Task Force on Patriot System Performance Report Summary,* 20301–3140 (January 2005), *http://www.acq.osd.mil/dsb/reports/ADA435837.pdf.*

autonomous systems.[35] Cognitive human enhancement may also play a role. Ultimately, militaries will have to balance the risks associated with delegating too much authority—whether to people or autonomous systems—and running the risk of undesired action on the battlefield vs. withholding authority and risking moving too slowly to respond to enemy action. There is no easy answer to this problem, but technology that quickens the pace of battle is likely to force it to be an even more significant dilemma in the future.

Shaping the Perceptions of Key Populations

Technologies can aid in the conduct of war, but war is fought by people. Maintaining the support of key populations has always been critical in war. In guerrilla wars and insurgencies, influencing the civilian population is a direct aim of both sides, but even in nation-state conflicts domestic support is crucial to sustaining the campaign. Militaries have often sought, as both sides did in World War II, to sap the will of the enemy population, either through propaganda or even direct attacks.

The radical democratization of communications brought about by social media, the internet, blogs, and ubiquitous smartphones has increased the diversity of voices and the volume and pace of information being exchanged, altering the way in which actors compete to influence populations. In a pre-internet era, mass communications were the province of only a few organizations—governments and major media organizations. Even in democratic countries, there were only a handful of major newspaper and television outlets. Information technology and the advent of many-to-many communications has shifted the media landscape, however. Any person can now gain a nationwide or international following on YouTube, Twitter, or any number of other social media venues. Governments and non-state groups are already leveraging these tools to their benefit. Jihadist videos showing attacks—both for propaganda and instructional purposes—are available on YouTube. Russia has deployed an army of Twitter bots to spread its propaganda.[36] The Islamic State similarly employs a sophisticated network of human Twitter users to spread its messages.[37]

Various conflict actors, state and non-state alike, will seek to leverage new media tools as well as old media to help spread their messages. While states generally have more resources at their disposal, the net effect of the widespread availability of social media is to increase the relative power of non-state groups, whose messaging tools are now far more capable than twenty years ago. This means that even in conflicts between nation-states, messaging directly to various publics—the enemy's, one's own, and third parties—may be critical to influencing perceptions of legitimacy, victory, and resolve.

STRATEGIC AGILITY: A STRATEGY FOR MANAGING DISRUPTIVE CHANGE

How should the U.S. military prepare for these potential disruptive changes in warfare? While investments in key technology areas are important, the U.S. defense budget is insufficient, even in the best of times, to invest in every possible game-changing opportunity. Moreover, technology alone will rarely lead to paradigm shifts in warfare without the right concepts for use. To sustain American military dominance, the Department of Defense should pursue a strategy of strategic agility, with a focus on increasing the DOD's ability to rapidly respond to disruptive changes in warfare.[38] Rapid reaction capabilities, modular design, and experimentation are critical components of achieving strategic agility.

Rapid reaction capabilities

U.S. military forces have evolved considerably since the Cold War, but the nation remains saddled with a Cold War-era bureaucracy that is too sluggish to respond

---

[35] John K. Hawley, "Not by Widgets Alone: The Human Challenge of Technology-intensive Military Systems," *Armed Forces Journal*, February 1, 2011, *http://www.armedforcesjournal .com/not-by-widgets-alone/*.

[36] Lawrence Alexander, "Social Network Analysis Reveals Full Scale of Kremlin's Twitter Bot Campaign," *GlobalVoices.org*, April 2, 2015, *https://globalvoices.org/2015/04/02/analyzing-kremlin-twitter-bots/* and Lawrence Alexander, "The Curious Chronology of Russian Twitter Bots," *GlobalVoices.org*, April 27, 2015, *https://globalvoices.org/2015/04/27/the-curious-chro-nology-of-russian-twitter-bots/*. For an interesting survey of Twitter bot activity and analysis of a specific application, see Stefanie Haustein et al., "Tweets as impact indicators: Examining the implications of automated 'bot' accounts on Twitter," *http://arxiv.org/pdf/1410.4139.pdf*.

[37] Jared Cohen, "Digital Counterinsurgency: How to Marginalize the Islamic State Online," *Foreign Affairs* (November/December 2015), *https://www.foreignaffairs.com/articles/middle-east/digital-counterinsurgency*.

[38] Richard Danzig, *Driving in the Dark Ten Propositions About Prediction and National Security (Washington DC: Center for a New American Security, 2011)*.

to the pace of change of modern warfare. The DOD's capability development process proved wholly inadequate to respond to emergent needs in Iraq and Afghanistan, necessitating the creation of ad hoc standalone processes and task forces, such as the MRAP Task Force, ISR Task Force, JIEDDO [Joint Improvised Threat Defeat Agency], Rapid Equipping Force, Joint Rapid Acquisition Cell, and other entities.[39] While the specific capabilities that these groups fielded may not be needed in future wars, the need for rapid reaction capabilities is universal. In fact, rapidly responding to enemy innovations is likely to be even more critical in major nation-state wars than in counterinsurgencies, which often play out over longer time horizons and at lower violence levels. DOD should move to institutionalize many of the ad hoc processes developing during the most recent wars and ensure the Department is better prepared for rapid adaptability in future conflicts.

Modular design

Even as DOD pursues more rapid reaction capabilities, major platforms such as submarines, aircraft carriers, aircraft, and tanks will still have lifespans measured in decades. In order to ensure their continuing utility, modularity should be front and center in their design, with the platform conceived of as a "truck" to carry various weapon systems that can be more easily upgraded over time. In practice, this modular design principle is already in use in many weapon systems throughout the U.S. military, from the F–16 to the B–52 to the M–1 tank, all of which have had many upgrades over the course of their lifespan. Some platforms are inherently modular, such as aircraft carriers, which carry aircraft that then project combat power.[40] This principle of modularity, which emphasizes "payloads over platforms" should be expanded to include "software over payloads" as well, allowing rapid technology refresh to keep pace with the information revolution.

Furthermore, modular design can evolve entirely beyond the platform, as the DARPA SOSITE program does, emphasizing the weapon system as a collection of plug-and-play platforms that can be upgraded over time. This concept places a greater burden on protected communications between distributed system elements. When successful, however, this concept allows even more rapid technology refresh as individual platform elements can be replaced individually without redesigning the entire weapon system, upgrading combat capability incrementally and at lower cost.

Experimentation

In 1943, Lieutenant General Lesley McNair, then Commander of Army Ground Forces, sent a memorandum to the Chief of Staff of the Army arguing for reducing armor-centric units in favor of making tanks subordinate to infantry. LTG McNair explained that the success of the German blitzkrieg was, in his mind, an aberration and that the proper role of tanks was "to exploit the success of our infantry."[41] The fact that there remained significant debates within the U.S. Army as late as 1943, *after* Germany had decisively demonstrated the effectiveness of armored forces in Europe, shows the importance of doctrine in exploiting paradigm shifts in warfare. New technologies alone rarely accrue significant battlefield advantage if they are not used in combination with new concepts of operation, training, doctrine, and organization.

From a training perspective, the U.S. military currently retains many advantages over potential adversaries; however, that also means others have more room for improvement. When it comes to embracing new doctrinal or organizational shifts, however, U.S. military dominance may actually be a weakness. U.S. organizations

---

[39] Mine Resistant Ambush Protected Vehicle (MRAP) Task Force; Intelligence Surveillance and Reconnaissance (ISR) Task Force; Joint Improvised Explosive Device Defeat Organization (JIEDDO). For more on these and other rapid capability processes, see Department of Defense, "Report of the Defense Science Board Task Force on Fulfillment of Urgent Operational Needs," July 2009, *http://www.acq.osd.mil/dsb/reports/ADA503382.pdf;* Christopher J. Lamb, Matthew J. Schmidt, and Berit G. Fitzsimmons, "MRAPs, Irregular Warfare, and Pentagon Reform," *Institute for National Strategic Studies,* Occasional Paper 6, June 2009, *http://usacac.army.mil/cac2/cgsc/sams/media/MRAPs.pdf;* and Ashton B. Carter, "Running the Pentagon Right," *Foreign Affairs,* January/February 2014, *https://www.foreignaffairs.com/articles/unitedstates/2013–12–06/running-pentagon-right.*

[40] Jerry Hendrix, *Retreat from Range: The Rise and Fall of Carrier Aviation* (Washington DC: Center for a New American Security, 2015).

[41] Kent Roberts Greenfield, Robert R. Palmer and Bell I. Wiley, *United States Army in World War II, The Army Ground Forces, The Organization of Ground Combat Troops* (Washington, D.C.: U.S. Government Printing Office, 1947), 319–335, *http://www.history.army.mil/html/books/002/2–1/CMH_Pub_2–1.pdf.* See also Kenneth Steadman, "The Evolution of the Tank in the U.S. Army," Combat Studies Institute: U.S. Army Command and General Staff College, April 21, 1982.

heavily invested in current ways of warfighting may be slow to adapt to disruptive changes.[42] A rigorous and deliberate program of experimentation is critical to uncovering new ways of warfighting and breaking out of pre-conceive doctrinal paradigms.

Experiments differ from training or unit qualification as the purpose of experiments is to try new ideas, fail, adapt, and try again in order to learn how new technologies change warfare. The U.S. military currently lacks sufficient depth in experimentation, which is critical to sustaining U.S. military advantage in the face of disruptive change. The ability to rapidly adjust not only the hardware and digital software comprising military power, but also the human software—the training, doctrine, concepts of operation, and organizations—is likely to be the most critical factor in ensuring long-term advantage.

CONCLUSION

The twentieth century saw a number of major disruptive changes in warfare, with the introduction of machine guns, tanks, aircraft, submarines, nuclear weapons, GPS, stealth, guided munitions, and communications networks all changing how militaries fought in war. The penalty for nations that failed to adapt to these changes was high. While the United States weathered these changes and in many cases led them, future success is not guaranteed. The proliferation of existing advanced technologies around the globe and the continued unfolding of the information revolution will drive further changes in how militaries fight. To be best prepared for the changes to come, the U.S. military should pursue strategic agility, supported by rapid reaction capabilities, modular design, and experimentation to rapidly respond to disruptive change. While the specific shape of the future is uncertain, the need to adapt to the challenges to come is universal.

Chairman MCCAIN. Dr. Singer?

STATEMENT OF DR. PETER W. SINGER, STRATEGIST AND SENIOR FELLOW, NEW AMERICA

Dr. SINGER. Chairman McCain, Ranking Member Reed, distinguished members of the committee, thank you for inviting me to join you here today. It is a deep honor.

I am a defense analyst who has written nonfiction books on various emerging topics of importance to the series from private military contractors to drones and robotics to cybersecurity to my new book "Ghost Fleet: A Novel of the Next World War," which combines nonfiction style research with a fictionalized scenario of a 21st century great power conflict to explore the future of war.

This choice of scenario is deliberate as while terrorism and Middle East insurgencies are not going away, we face a return to the most serious kind of national security concern that shaped the geopolitics of the last century, great power competition, which could spill into actual conflict, either by accident or choice. In turn, the scale of such a challenge demonstrates the stakes at hand which hopefully we will not have to wait for to drive change.

In my written submission, I cover five key areas that distinguish the future of war, most especially in a great power context and needed actions we need to take from recognizing the challenges of new domains of conflict in space and cyberspace, to dealing with our pattern of buying what I call the Pontiac Azteks of war, defense programs that are over-promised, over-engineered, and end up overpriced.

But in my remarks today, I would like to focus on one important issue, the new technology race at hand.

---

[42] Paul Scharre, "How to Lose the Robotics Revolution," War on the Rocks, July 29, 2014, *http://warontherocks.com/2014/07/how-to-lose-the-robotics-revolution/*.

Since 1945, U.S. defense planning has focused on having a qualitative edge to overmatch our adversaries, planning to be a generation ahead in technology and capability. This assumption has become baked into everything from our overall defense strategy all the way down to small unit tactics.

Yet U.S. forces cannot count on that overmatch in the future. Mass campaigns of state-linked intellectual property theft has meant we are paying much of the research and development costs for our adversaries. These challengers are also growing their own cutting-edge technology. China, for example, just overtook the EU [European Union] in national R&D spending and is on pace to match the U.S. in 5 years, with new projects ranging from the world's fastest supercomputers to three different long-range drone strike programs. Finally, off-the-shelf technologies can be bought to rival even the most advanced tools in the U.S. arsenal.

This is crucial as not just are many of our most long-trusted, dominant platforms from warships to warplanes vulnerable to new classes of weapons now in more conflict actors' hands but an array of potentially game-changing weapons lie just ahead in six key areas.

New generation of unmanned systems, both more diverse in size, shape, and form, but also more autonomous and more capable, meaning they can take on more roles from ISR to strike, flying off of anything from aircraft carriers to soldiers' hands.

Weapons that use not just the kinetics of a fist or the chemistry of gunpowder, but energy itself, ranging from electromagnetic railguns able to a fire projectile 100 miles to new directed energy systems that potentially reverse the cost equations of offense and defense.

Artificial intelligence, ubiquitous sensors, big data, and battle management systems that will redefine the observe, orient, and decide and act, the OODA loop.

Hypersonics, high speed rockets and missiles, 3-D printing technologies that threaten to do to the current defense marketplace what the iPod did to the music industry.

Human performance modification technologies that will reshape what is possible and maybe even what is proper in war.

The challenge, though, is the comparison that could be drawn between what is now or soon to be possible versus what are we actually buying today or planning to buy tomorrow. Our weapons modernization programs are too often not that modern. For example, if you start at the point of their conception, most of our top 10 programs of record are all old enough to vote for you, with several of them actually older than me.

We too often commit to mass buys before a system is truly tested, locking in on single major programs that are too big to fail and actually are not all that new. This dynamic shapes not just what we buy but extends their development time and ultimately our expectations of how much of it we will buy decades into the future, limiting our present and future flexibility. To abuse a metaphor, the growing per-unit cost of the cart is driving where we steer the horse.

At the heart of this is that while "disruption" is the new buzz word in defense thinking today, part of the Pentagon's new outreach to Silicon Valley, we struggle with the dual meaning of the concept. We claim to aspire for the new, but to be disrupted, the outdated must be discarded.

The roadblocks to disruption play at multiple levels, from specific weapons programs to organizational structures, to personnel systems and operating concepts. For instance, there is a long record of the Government funding exciting new projects that then wither away in that space between lab and program of record because they cannot supplant whatever old gear or program, factory, or internal tribe that is in the way. Indeed, there is even a term for it, the "valley of death." The same goes for all the new and important ideas and proposals you have heard in these hearings over the last several weeks. To be adopted, though, something will have to be supplanted.

As you program for the future, ultimately what you support in the new game-changers of not just programs but also thinking, structures, and organizations what you eliminate in the old and what you protect and nurture across that valley will matter more than any single additional plane or tank squeezed into a budget line item or OCO [overseas contingency operations] funding. It may even be the difference between the win or loss of a major war tomorrow.

I would like to close by offering two quotes that can serve hopefully as guideposts, one looking back and one forward.

The first is from the last interwar period where Churchill may have said it best. Quote: "Want of foresight, unwillingness to act when action would be simple and effective, lack of clear thinking, confusion of counsel until the emergency comes, until self-preservation strikes its jarring gong, these are the features which constitute the endless repetition of history."

The second is from a professor at China's National Defense University, arguing in a regime newspaper how his own nation should contemplate the future of war. Quote: "We must bear a third world war in mind when developing military forces." End quote.

We need to be mindful of both the lessons of the past but acknowledge the trends in motion and the real risks that loom in the future. That way we can take the needed steps to maintain deterrence and avoid miscalculation and, in so doing, keep the next world war where it belongs, in the realm of fiction.

Thank you.

[The prepared statement of Dr. Singer follows:]

PREPARED STATEMENT BY DR. PETER W. SINGER

THE LESSONS OF WORLD WAR 3

United States and Chinese warships battle at sea, firing everything from cannons to cruise missiles to lasers. Stealthy Russian and American fighter jets dogfight in the air, with robotic drones flying as their wingmen. Hackers in Shanghai and Silicon Valley duel in digital playgrounds. Fights in outer space decide who wins below on Earth.

Are theses scenes from a novel or what could actually take place in the real world the day after tomorrow? The answer is both.

Senator McCain, Senator Reed, thank you and the rest of the committee for inviting me here today. I am a defense analyst, who has written nonfiction books on various emerging topics of importance to the discussions in this series, ranging from private military contractors to drones and robotics to *cybersecurity*. Today I'd like to present a few of the lessons from my new book *Ghost Fleet: A Novel of the Next*

World War, which combines nonfiction style research with the fictionalized scenario of a 21st century great power conflict to explore the future of war.

OLD CONFLICT RISKS AND NEW STAKES

Great power conflicts defined the 20th century: two world wars claimed tens of millions of lives and the "cold" war that followed shaped everything from geopolitics to sports. At the start of the 21st century, however, the ever present fear of World War III was seemingly put into our historic rearview mirror. We went from worrying about powerful states to failed states, from a focus on the threats of organized national militaries to transnational networks of individual terrorists and insurgents. Indeed, just four years ago the *New York Times* published *an article* arguing the era of wars between states was over and that "War Really Is Going Out of Style."

If only it would. Today, with Russian landgrabs in the Ukraine and constant flights of bombers decorated with red stars probing Europe's borders, NATO is at its highest levels of alert since the mid 1980s. In the Pacific, China built more warships and warplanes than any other nation during the last several years, while the Pentagon has announced a strategy to "offset" it with a new generation of high-tech weapons.

Wars start through any number of pathways; one world war happened through deliberate action, the other a crisis that spun out of control. In the coming decades, a war might ignite accidentally, such as by two opposing warships trading paint near a reef not even marked on a nautical chart. Or it could slow burn and erupt as a reordering of the global system in the late 2020s, the period at which China's military build up is on pace to match the U.S.

Making either scenario more of a risk is that military planners and political leaders on all sides assume their side would be the one to win in a *"short"* and *"sharp"* fight, to use common phrases.

Let me be 100% clear, I do not think such a conflict is inevitable; though it is noteworthy that the *Communist Party's official People's Daily newspaper* warned that if the U.S. didn't change its policies in the Pacific, "A U.S.-China war is inevitable ... " While this may be a bit of posturing both for a U.S. and highly nationalist domestic audience (A 2014 poll by the Perth US–Asia center found that *74 percent of Chinese think their military would win in a war with the U.S.*), it illustrates further a simple but essential point: The global context is changing and what was once thinkable and then became unthinkable, is again thinkable.

For the committee's important work, it means our planning for deterrence and warfighting must recognize these risks, and the greater stakes. To give a historic parallel, it is the difference between the challenges that the British as a dominant global power in the last century faced in many of the very same places we find ourselves today, like Afghanistan and Iraq, versus the stakes and losses of World War One and Two.

MULTI-DOMAIN CONFLICT

A great power conflict would be quite different from the so-called "small wars" of today that the U.S. has grow accustomed to and, in turn, others think reveal a new American weakness. One of the key aspects is where it might take place, not in specific locations on a map like the South China sea, but in overall domains.

Unlike the Taliban, ISIS (Islamic State of Iraq and Syria), or even Saddam Hussein's Iraq, great powers can and will fight across all the domains. This will present new threats in areas whwre we've had unfettered access; indeed, the last time the U.S. fought a peer in the air or at sea was in 1945.

But a 21st century fight would also see battles for control of two new domains. The lifeblood of military communications and control now runs through space, meaning we would see humankind's first battles for the heavens. *Indeed, both China and Russia have anti-satellite weapons programs.* Similarly, we'd learn that "cyber war" is far more than stealing social security numbers or email from gossipy Hollywood executives, but *the takedown of the modern military nervous system and Stuxnet-style digital weapons causing physical damage.* Worrisome for the U.S. is that last year the Pentagon's weapons tester found *every single major weapons* program had "significant vulnerabilities" to cyber attack, while many of our newest weapons are powered by microchips increasingly designed and built by those they might face off against, opening up the *risks of hardware hacks.*

In both spaces, we have to focus more on building up resilience to achieve "deterrence by denial," taking away the potential fruits of any attack. This will require new innovative approaches, like networks of small, cheap satellites, rather than a small number of billion dollar points of failure, and new additions to our cybersecurity activities. This again is not merely a matter of greater spending, but being willing to explore new approaches and forgo our pattern of putting new challenges and capabilities into old boxes. For instance, there is much to learn from how Estonia went from being one of the first state victims of mass cyber attacks to one of the most secure against them, including through the creation of a Cyber Defense League.

A NEW RACE

Since 1945, U.S. defense planning has focused on having a qualitative edge to "overmatch" our adversaries, seeking to be a generation ahead in technology. This assumption has become baked into everything from our overall defense strategy all the way down to small unit tactics.

Yet U.S. forces can't count on that overmatch in the future. Mass campaigns of state-linked intellectual property theft has meant we are paying much of the research and development costs of our challengers (note the F–35 and J–31 fighter jet's similarity, for example). These challengers are also growing their own technology. *China, for example, just overtook the EU in R&D spending and is on pace to match the U.S. in five years,* with new projects ranging from the world's fastest supercomputers in the civilian space to three different long range drone strike programs on the military side. Finally, off-the-shelf technologies can be bought to rival even the most advanced tools in the U.S. arsenal. The winner of a recent robotics test, for instance, was not a U.S. defense contractor but a group of *South Korea student engineers.*

This is crucial as not just are many of our most long trusted platforms vulnerable to new classes of weapons, now in a wider array of conflict actors' hands, but an array of potentially game-changing weapons lie just ahead:

- A new generation of unmanned systems, both more diverse in size, shape, and form, but also more autonomous and more capable, meaning they can take on roles from ISR [Intelligence, Surveillance and Reconnaissance] to strike, flying from anything from aircraft carriers to soldier's hands.
- Weapons that operate using not the kinetics of a fist or gunpowder driving a bullet but energy itself, ranging from electromagnetic railgun, able to fire a projectile 100 miles, to new directed energy systems that potentially reverse the cost equations of offense and defense.
- Super long-range, and hyper fast air to air and air to ground missiles and strike systems.
- Artificial Intelligence, ubiquitous sensors, Big Data, and Battle Management systems that will redefine the observe, orient, decide and act (OODA) loop.
- 3–D printing technologies that threaten do to the current defense marketplace what the iPod did to the music industry.
- Human performance modification technologies that will reshape what is possible in the human side of war.

I would urge the committee and its staff to visit some of the various amazing government labs and facilities, from DARPA to the Office of Naval Research to Sandia to Air Force Research Lab, just to mention a few, where you can see firsthand how none of these science fiction sounding technologies are fictional.

The challenge, though, is the comparison that could be drawn between what is now or soon to be possible versus what we are actually buying today or planning to buy tomorrow. Our weapons modernization programs are too often not that modern. For example, if you start at their point of conception, most of our top 10 Programs of Record are old enough to vote, with a few actually older than me.

We too often commit to mass buys before a system is truly tested, locking in on single major programs that are "too big to fail" and actually aren't all that new. This dynamic shapes not just what we buy, but extends their development time, and ultimately our expectations of how much of that system we will buy decades into the future, limiting our present and future flexibility. To abuse a metaphor, the growing per unit costs of the cart drives where we steer the horse.

At the heart of this failing dynamic is that while "disruption" is a new buzzword in defense thinking today, part of the Pentagon's new outreach to Silicon Valley, we struggle with the dual meaning in the concept: We claim to aspire for the new, but to be disrupted, the outdated must also be discarded. Amazon didn't merely pioneer online book sales, but it also ended the business of most brick and mortar bookstores.

The roadblocks to disruption exist at multiple levels, from specific weapons programs to organizational change and operating concepts. For instance, there is a long record of the government funding exciting new projects that then wither away in that space between lab and program of record because they can't supplant whatever old gear or program, factory, or internal tribe that is in the way. Indeed, there is even a term for it: the "Valley of Death." The same goes for all the new and important concepts you have heard about in these hearings over the last few weeks. To be adapted, something will have to be supplanted.

As you program for the future, ultimately what you support in the new gamechangers of not just programs, but also thinking, structures and organizations, what you eliminate in the old, and what you protect and nurture across that "Valley" will matter more than any single additional plane or tank squeezed into a budget line item or OCO funding. It may be the difference between the win or loss of a major war tomorrow.

THE PONTIAC AZTEKS OF WAR

The issue, though, is not just one of pursuing new innovations, but that we too often plan for the best in the future of war, not expect the worst.

A key challenge here is our defense acquisition systems has specialized in designing, building, and buying the Pontiac Azteks of war. The Aztek, which debuted in 2001, was a car that optimistically tried to be everything—a sports car, a minivan and an SUV [Sport Untility Vehicle]. Instead, it ended up overengineered, overpriced and overpromised. There is an array of Pentagon programs today with similar characteristics. We optimistically and unrealistically planned for them to be good at all types of war, but they risk being unequal to many of our new challenges.

For example, in the air, we are in the midst of buying jet fighters with shorter range than their World War II equivalents three generations back and *a tanker aircraft that lacks the defensive systems for anything above a "medium threat" environment*, at the very moment a potential adversary is developing longer reach to target both their bases and themselves in an air to air fight. At sea, we are embarking on a buying program for a warship that the Navy's own tester says is *"not expected to be survivable in high-intensity combat."*

There are deep dangers of this kind of "fingers crossed" planning. What will it be like in the 2020s to fly a fighter jet conceived in the 1990s that happens to get in a dogfight or is called upon to do close air support? That leaders in 2015 argued such situations wouldn't happen will be little aid to that pilot. What happens if an adversary decides not to play by our rules and raises the fight above "medium threat" level? What happens to a crew that goes into battle in a ship "next expected to be survivable" for the battle?

My hope is that in helping the U.S. military prepare for the future, this committee constantly looks to the potential worst day of he future of war, not the best.

CHALLENGE THE ASSUMPTIONS

From the rise of great powers to the introduction of new classes of technology to waves of globalization, we are living through a series of sweeping changes that impact the fundamental where, when, how, and even who of war. Child soldiers, drone pilots, and hackers all now play a role in war. Still, especially given the overreach of acolytes of network-centric warfare during the last 1990s drawdown (who argued that technology would somehow solve all our problems, *"lifting the fog of war"*), it must be noted that nothing changes the *why* of war—our human flaws and mistakes still drive conflict, whether it is fought with a stone or a drone.

Nor does it mean that we can ignore the historic lessons of war, where we repeatedly fall prey to what HR McMaster has described as *key "myths" of war*. War will never be perfect. Indeed, when military aircraft gained widespread adoption in the 1920s, a new breed of thinkers like Billy Mitchell and Giulio Douhet claimed that there would be no more need for old ground armies. Yet the need for "boots on the ground" lived on throughout the 20th century—just as it will live on into the 21st.

Such caveats are not to say that the new technologies like the tank or the airplane weren't fundamental shifts in the last century or that the dynamic shifts should be ignored in ours. If the United States wants to hold on to its grip on the top, just spending more is no longer sustainable, nor the right answer. Much as both military and civilian leaders in the British Empire had to rethink their assumptions about the world, our old assumptions need to be re-examined today.

We must be open to change across the system, from rethinking how we conduct professional military education (such as by making the war college more competitive and encouraging and rewarding more externships to diversify thinking and exposure to new technologies and concepts) to re-examining the very roles we envision for weapons. Just as the B–52 went being conceived as a strategic nuclear bomber to offering powerful close air support capabilities, we might see everything from submarines gaining new utility by becoming more akin to aircraft carriers for unmanned air and sea systems or long range strike bombers complicating enemy access denial plans by taking on roles once handled by jet fighters and AWACs [Airborne Warning and Control System] and RPA [Robotic Process Automation] controllers. Much is possible, if we allow ourselves to break free of the status quo and experiment our way into the future.

To continue that Interwar years parallel, we will benefit from programs more akin to the Louisiana Maneuvers and Fleet Problem exercises that broke new ground and helped discover the next generation of both technology and human talent, rather than an approach that focuses on validating present capabilities and approaches and/or making allies feel better about themselves.

Any true change will be uncomfortable, of course, as there will be winners and losers in everything from the defense marketplace to personnel systems. It is to be expected that necessary change will inevitably be resisted, sometimes for valid reasons, sometimes for reasons that have nothing to do with battlefield performance. For instance, the British not only invented the tank and used it successfully in World War I, but they carried out a series of innovative tests during the interwar years on the famous Salisbury plain that showed just how game-changing tanks could be in the next conflict. Yet the British veered away from fully adapting to the *Blitzkrieg* concept they arguably birthed, largely because of the consequences that implementing it would have had on the cherished regimental system that was at the center of British *military culture.* This was not just a British pheonomenon; as late as 1939, the head of the U.S. Cavalry, *Maj. Gen. John Knowles Herr* was testifying to Congress about the superiority of horse forces and resisting the shift to mechanized units. We should be mindful of any parallels today. This resistance will sometime be direct and sometimes be behind the scenes, including by claiming never to be satisfied budget wants prevent change, when that is what should be causing it.

In this time of strategic and technologic shift, my hope is that the committee will be constantly challenging the status quo and the underlying assumptions about what is and is not changing.

CONCLUSIONS

There are two quotes that can serve as guide posts in this effort, one looking back and one forward. The first is from the last interwar period, where Churchill may have said it best: "Want of foresight, unwillingness to act when action would be simple and effective, lack of clear thinking, confusion of counsel until the emergency comes, until self-preservation strikes its jarring gong—these are the features which constitute the endless repetition of history."

The second is from a professor at China's National Defense University, arguing in a regime newspaper how his own nation should contemplate the future of war: *"We must bear a third world war in mind when developing military forces."*

We need to be mindful of both the lessons of the past, but also acknowledge the trends in motion and the real risks that loom in the future. That way we can take the needed steps to maintain deterrence and avoid miscalculation, and in so doing, keep the next world war where it belongs, in the realm of fiction.

Biography

Peter Warren Singer is Strategist and Senior Fellow at New America, a nonpartisan thinktank based in Washington DC. New America's funding, including full list of donors and amounts can be found at: *https://www.newamerica.org/contribute/#our-funding-section.*

Singer is also the author of multiple bestselling and award-winning books, including most recently *Ghost Fleet: A Novel of the Next World War,* an editor at *Popular Science,* where he runs the *Eastern Arsenal blog on Chinese military technology,* and a consultant for the U.S. military, intelligence community, and entertainment industry. Further background at *www.pwsinger.com.*

Chairman MCCAIN. Thank you very much, Doctor.

General Alexander, you mentioned that the legislation that was recently passed on cyber was a good step forward. What more?

General ALEXANDER. Chairman, I think the key thing that has to be clear in that legislation, that when there is a military response required from actions that that has to go immediately to the Defense Department. What I am concerned about is we set up a process that it is delayed at the Department of Homeland Security, inspected, and then sent. So how long does that inspection take? For metadata, we could do that automatically.

So what I would encourage is the development of a set of standards—think of these as protocols—where both houses in Congress could agree that these type of information hold no personally identifiable information and is necessary for the protection of the Nation, and it could go directly to all the parties. So I am not saying cut DHS [Department of Homeland Security] out. I am saying ensure that DOD gets it in real time. It would be analogous to a radar, and instead of DOD getting the radar feed on where the missile is, that goes to DHS and then they tell you where the missile is.

Chairman MCCAIN. You said it is important to partner with industry. I get the impression that industry is not particularly interested in partnering with us.

General ALEXANDER. I think there are two parts to that. You know, it has been an exciting year and a half out. What I have found is industry is very much into cybersecurity. They are very concerned about what they share with the Government because of liability. But at the end of the day, they recognize that the Government is the only one that could defend them from a nation state-like attack.

Chairman MCCAIN. Dr. Singer, is the F-35 the last manned fighter aircraft in your view?

Dr. SINGER. I do not know if it is the last because certainly other people may continue to construct them. We may as well. The question is, to make a historic parallel, its comparison, if we are thinking about the interwar years, the Spitfire or, to use a Navy example, the Wildcat systems that the investment prove worthwhile, or does it parallel the Gloster Gladiator, the last best biplane? I would offer to the committee to explore that parallel history of a program that we set the requirements. The requirements were set early, and then the world changed around it. So all the things that seemed fantastic and useful about the Gladiator—it was a metal biplane. It carried two machine guns. It could go faster than previous biplanes. It was outdated before it even left the development cycle. But they continued to push forward with it. Its nickname among pilots who flew it in World War II was not the Gladiator but it was nicknamed the "flying coffin."

Chairman MCCAIN. Some other aircraft have inherited that moniker as well.

Dr. SINGER. So I think the challenge is going to be—we will buy the F-35. I think we are going to have to wrestle with, obviously, the issues that you have pointed out, the per-unit costs, how that will affect in the long term our plans for how many we want to buy. I have a hard time believing that in the year 2025 or 2030 we are still going to be buying the same numbers that we expect to buy now. The world will have changed. The capabilities will have changed. Also its integration with unmanned systems and what role will it play or will it be able to play in terms of partnering with unmanned systems or managing them. So there is a sea of change.

My worry is that it is a program that many of the concepts for it were set, to put it bluntly, the year that I was leaving college.

Chairman MCCAIN. Mr. Scharre, we all agree that the Pentagon is not structured nor is the command system structured now to meet the new challenges that you witnesses have aptly described. Take a stab at how should we restructure the Pentagon to meet these new challenges.

Mr. SCHARRE. Thank you, Mr. Chairman.

I think one important disconnect that has come to light in the last 15 years is the disconnect between what the Pentagon is doing in terms of long-term acquisition and very near-term needs in the combatant commands. We saw this in Iraq and Afghanistan, the creation of all of these ad hoc processes like MRAP [Mine Resistant Ambush Protected Vehicle] task force, an ISR [Intelligence, Surveillance, Reconnaissance] task force, and JIEDDO [Joint Improvised-Threat Defeat Agency], things that were basically silver bullets the Secretary had to personally fire at a problem to get it fixed. So institutionalizing that is important not just for counterinsurgency or guerilla wars, perhaps even more importantly for major wars where the level of violence is likely to be higher and the timelines are shorter and the need to rapidly innovate in a battlefield is really essential, as well as to anticipate these problems.

The Department has made some steps in that direction with the creation of things like a joint emergent operational needs sort of pathway to create requirements. But I think there is a lot more to be done in terms of giving the COCOM's a voice, in terms of near-term capability development, and then creating a pathway. The services have some of these individually—the Air Force does—to do rapid capability development.

Chairman MCCAIN. Mr. Clark?

Mr. CLARK. Yes, sir. So I would say that we need to look at having one process that is how we develop the requirements and acquire large manned acquisition programs, so ships, aircraft, where we might want to have a more deliberate process by which we develop the requirements because of the need for them to last several decades and potentially protect large numbers of people onboard. Then have a separate process like Mr. Scharre is talking about where we acquire smaller programs, so everything below that which is 99 percent of the programs that we develop in DOD where we can develop the requirements in concert with a technology demonstration and prototype program. A lot of the technologies that new acquisition programs leverage are already mature and sitting, waiting at the valley of death to make the trip across. So they are waiting for some boat to come and pick them up and carry them there. Well, we could take advantage of and bridge that valley if we instead said everything that is not a large manned platform, for example, weapons sensors, unmanned vehicles, et cetera, is able to take advantage of an acquisition process where we develop requirements at the same time as we develop the specifications and the plan for the system. So it would merge requirements and acquisition to a much greater degree.

Chairman MCCAIN. So we would not need a 1,000-page document for a new handgun.

Mr. CLARK. Exactly. New handgun, new unmanned system, all of those technologies are ones we are going to harvest from industry or DOD labs that have already been developed. So why not just create a process that develops the specifications that we actually want in the final program very quickly based on what has already been achieved technically and we know what the cost is going to be.

Chairman MCCAIN. Thank you.

Senator Reed?

Senator REED. Well, thank you very much, Mr. Chairman.

Thank you, gentlemen, for your very, very insightful testimony.

It strikes me that we are talking about, as many of you mentioned, this disconnect between the reality that we all recognize today, even the leaders in the Defense Department and my colleagues here, and operational practice, institutional outlooks, the equipment, the training, everything. The question is how in very real time, quick time we sync those things up.

One thought is by having exercises where we actually game this out in a comprehensive way. I am recalling—someone mentioned the interwar years where—and the chairman mentioned the development of the carrier, et cetera. That was done when people were sitting at the War College in Newport thinking very carefully about the threats, the new technology, and providing a basis. So where are we in the process of sort of forcing the system by having comprehensive exercises that will force us to answer specific questions like how do we organize or reorganize. What equipment do we really need, et cetera?

General Alexander, you can start and then I ask all the witnesses.

General ALEXANDER. Senator, I think the first thing that we have to look at is to expand our outlook on what cyber can do to our country. I think in the military, we focused on military-on-military engagements. But practically speaking, an adversary is going to go after our civilian infrastructure first. You know, on war, when people talk about total war, take the will of the people out to fight. We are seeing that in some of the things going on today. Take down the power grid and the financial sector, and everybody is going to forget about these problems. We are essentially isolated. So I think we have to step back and look at this in a more comprehensive manner. What does it mean for the Defense Department to really protect the Nation in this area.

I think there is a great start with the way the teams have been set up and what they can do, but there is a long way to go. I do think we have to have this war game.

During my tenure at Cyber Command, some of the questions came up. Do we go from sub-unified to unified to separate service where folks like Petraeus and Stavridis said go to a separate service. I was not there, but I do think we have to step into this area. Secretary Gates had some great insights on so how are we going to do this because it is a new way of thinking about warfare where our Nation now is at risk. In the past, we could easily separate out the military to overseas and what went on in the country as others. In this area, you cannot do that because the first thing they are going to go after is our civilian infrastructure.

So I think the war game has got to start with that and how we respond to that. It is going to escalate at orders of magnitude faster than any other form of warfare that we have seen.

Senator REED. Thank you.

Please, Mr. Clark.

Mr. CLARK. Senator, I would say looking at the interwar years is a great example because what we did back then is the warfighters would get together at Sims Hall up at the Naval War College and play out the war game on the floor there with play ships and models and everything and then go out and do a series of battle experiments at sea to practice the best of breed concepts that came out of that process.

So right now, the Department of Defense is reinvigorating its war-gaming efforts in an effort to try to put the intellectual capital into the development of new warfighting concepts. Then those warfighting concepts that emerge from those, the best of breed, if you will, for how they are going to fight in the future—then they need to be taken out, as you are saying, and experimented with in exercises using real systems in a real operating environment.

I would say one other thing that DOD does not do well, which they need to start doing a better job of, is incorporating technologists into these discussions. So we run a war game. We get a bunch of operators together and we give them a problem and they know their systems that they have today from the ship or aircraft they just left, and they go play it out and figure out the best way to fight. But they are not taking advantage of what technology might offer them in the next 5 or 10 years, which is really the timeframe we are aiming for. So we need to bring into those war games, into the subsequent experiments the technology experts that know where technology is going but do not necessarily know how it is going to be used. By putting those two groups of people together, you are more likely to get an operational concept that comes out it that is able to leverage new technologies and do something different than what we did before.

The examples of the past where we had stealth or where we developed passive sonar are perfect examples of where our technology people came in and said, well, this is possible. Operators said, well, I think I know how I would use that, and they came up with a way to apply it. Then we could take that out in the field and practice it. That is something DOD needs to do a better job of.

Senator REED. Mr. Scharre, my time is diminishing. So your comments, please.

Mr. SCHARRE. Yes. Thanks, Mr. Senator.

I guess I could not agree more that this process of experimentation is really critical. I would just add that it has to be segregated from training in terms of qualifying a unit. When we send in Army units something like NTC [National Training Center], that is about ensuring the unit's readiness and training. There may be room for actually taking some units—we have done them in the past—and setting them aside as experimental units to try new concepts, and that is something that the Department should be looking at.

Senator REED. Thank you.

Dr. Singer, finally.

Dr. SINGER. Very rapidly. I think the challenge in the existing system is the exercises either are about validating existing concepts—you hear the phrase often "getting back to basics." What if the basics have changed in the interim—or they are about allies, making allies feel better them about themselves, partnership capacity building and confidence building. That is different than the interwar years of the Louisiana maneuvers and the fleet problem exercises.

Secondly, those were very valuable in the interwar years not just in showing what to buy and how to use it but the "who," what kind of personnel thrive in these new styles of war. So it is linking the exercises to your personnel system.

Third, rapidly, a quick issue is the budget is not a preventative of it. They went through the Great Depression and figured out aircraft carriers, amphibious landing. It is often culture of implementation.

Then finally, beware in this of the lessons and the people saying they are adopt but only in an uneven manner. I think that, to circle back to the cybersecurity aspect, is a challenge here where we are taking a lot of new capabilities and putting some of them into old boxes. So we have built up Cyber Command, but we still have a system where the Pentagon's own weapons tester found, in their words, significant vulnerabilities in every single major weapons system.

Senator REED. Thank you.

I assume, if someone disagrees, that General Alexander's comment is that this is much broader than the Department of Defense and we tend to look ourselves in sort of stovepipes of defense planning, et cetera. But this has to be a usually comprehensive exercise involving the Federal Reserve, the Department of Defense, the major utilities, everyone engaged. I assume everyone agrees with that.

Thank you, Mr. Chairman.

Chairman MCCAIN. Senator Inhofe?

Senator INHOFE. Thank you, Mr. Chairman.

First of all, General Alexander, I appreciate the time we had. I learned a lot in the time that we spent together when you were in your position. It was very meaningful.

I recall when I was first elected—I came from the House to the Senate—I replaced David Boren. David Boren was the chairman of the Intelligence Committee. He told me at that time one of the problems that we were never able to deal with was the fact that we have all of this technology and all these things that we are finding out, and yet we seem to be competing with ourselves. I mean, you have the FBI, the CIA [Central Intelligence Agency], the NSA—we did not have Homeland Security then.

But I am kind of seeing the same thing. Well, we made some headway there. In fact, up in Tuzla during the Bosnia thing, was the first time all of the entities I mentioned were in one room together. At least they were talking.

Now, you mentioned in your statement commercial and private entities cannot afford to defend themselves alone against nation state attacks nor nation state-like attacks in cyberspace and that the U.S. Government is the only one that can and should fire back.

Now, it just seems to me that we had that—I would ask you what agency—how this should be restructured because we have each one of these like the NSA. They have a cyber division and the CIA and all that. How would you envision—and I know you have given some thought to this—restructuring this thing to be more effective?

General ALEXANDER. Well, I am going to take from what I talked with Secretary Gates about because I think he had the greatest insights. When you look at the departments that are responsible for protecting the country in this space, you have Homeland Security. You have the Department of Justice, and you have the Department of Defense. Practically speaking, all the technical talent really lies at NSA in deep technical expertise in the network, and hence the reason we put Cyber Command there so you married those two pieces up.

The FBI has some great talent for domestic capabilities, but they do not have any of the deep technical talent that came out of World War II for encryption, decryption, and the things that really helped the network operate. So when you talk about network operations, that is probably the best expertise.

So I think as you look at it, the question then becomes what do you do that brings those three departments together. He looked at a third hat. I would ask you to reach out to him and get his thoughts on it. I know he has testified once, but he had some great insights and I think directly from him on that, what is probably the best approach. We actually started down that road and fell apart at one point. But I think that is where our country needs to get to because that allows you to look at what you are going to do to defend the Nation and what you are going to do to recover when bad things happen. Both of those have to be synchronized as we go forward.

Specifically it goes back to what Senator Reed brought out. If our Nation is attacked and they take down the power grid and they do massive damage, where is your first priority for the future of the Nation is something that has to be, well, how am I going to defend this country, first and foremost has to be put on the table. So those kind of decisions have to be made. I think that is what I would do.

I am not sure—I have not been able to think of a way of collapsing all the intel agencies together unless you just smashed them all together under the DNI [Director of National Intelligence] and then made some agencies. But you are actually back to where you are today. So I do not know a better way right off the top of my head to do that, Senator.

Senator INHOFE. I was going to bring up the effort that you made in that position like going out to the University of Tulsa, and they developed a great program there. As Dr. Singer mentioned, we have to watch what the Chinese and others are doing, the emphasis they are putting on, they are teaching their kids. I look down the road and think they are passing us up everywhere.

Let me just real quickly get back to the fact that a statement that was made by Bob Gates talking about how we have never once gotten it right. I can remember the last year I served on the House Armed Services Committee was 1994. I recall when we had experts testifying, and one of them said that in 10 years we will no longer need ground troops. Well, that is kind of an example of what is out there in a reality that we have not been getting it right.

But one thing I think that Bob Gates got right was when he was on the panel. Incidentally, we have had great panels the last 3 weeks and up to and including this panel of experts. We had the people in think tanks. We also had the five professors from different universities. We had them all responding to the fact that Bob Gates stated that in 1961 we spent—defending America consumed 51 percent of our budget. Today it is 15 percent of our budget.

In all the problems that you are addressing that you have been talking about—and I would ask all of you this question—are we not giving the right emphasis to defending America? Right now with sequestration coming on, they are insisting on having an equal amount of money affecting the social programs as defending America. So do you think that we need to—you can just say yes or no, going down the table—reprioritize making defending America the number one priority again? Dr. Singer?

Dr. SINGER. Sequestration is incredibly unstrategic, but it is akin to shooting yourself in the foot not shooting yourself in the head. So how we deal with it will determine success or failure.

Senator INHOFE. I think that is yes.

Mr. Scharre?

Mr. SCHARRE. Thank you, Senator.

I acknowledge there are some very difficult domestic political compromises here, but I think it is very clear that we certainly are not spending enough on defense today in order to defend the country adequately.

Senator INHOFE. Thank you.

Mr. Clark?

Mr. CLARK. Yes.

Senator INHOFE. Thank you, Mr. Chairman.

Chairman MCCAIN. Senator Manchin?

Senator MANCHIN. Thank you, Mr. Chairman.

Thank all of you for being here today.

General Alexander, if I could ask, which country or which group has the most to gain from attacking—the cyber attack to America? Russia, China, ISIL? Who do you rate as the number one?

General ALEXANDER. So each of them have different objectives. But Russia—when we disagreed on the Crimea, we saw increased attacks against companies like Target and Home Depot from their hackers.

Senator MANCHIN. How would that benefit them as a country?

General ALEXANDER. Well, they allow their hackers kind of freedom. They can say, okay, you guys can go do this. We are not watching. Go have a good time. They steal. They make money. We get hurt. Russia kind of sends an indirect message.

The same thing in Iran. When you look at the disruptive attacks on Wall Street, what they are doing is they are sending a message. You have sanctioned us in the finance and the energy sector. We will fire back. Saudi Aramco, your energy sector.

In China, it is different. China is all about building their economy. All they are doing is stealing everything they can to grow their economy. It is intellectual property. It is our future. I think it is the greatest transfer of wealth in history. Interestingly, we could stop that. I believe that. I really do.

I think, Senator, if I could, what Senator Reed and Senator Inhofe brought up, if you put those two together and said why do we not have a major exercise with industry in there, industry is willing to pay their portion for cyber defense. I am convinced of that. If they did their part right in defending what they need to do in setting up the ability to tell the Nation when they are under attack, you could stop attacks from Iran, Russia, and China, and we should do that.

Senator MANCHIN. Let me ask you about the NSA. We are talking about all this outside interest in attacking the United States for many, many reasons you just stated. What have they done to stop the Edward Snowdens of the NSA from inside attacks?

General ALEXANDER. So we set up a program in 2013 to look at all the things that——

Senator MANCHIN. Was it a surprise to you? I am so sorry to interrupt you. A surprise to you have this happen. I know you were there.

General ALEXANDER. I was surprised at a person who we had entrusted to move data from one server to another really was not trustworthy.

Senator MANCHIN. You had him at a high level. I mean, you knew you had him at a very sensitive, high level, and you did not vetting him well enough?

General ALEXANDER. No. His level was exaggerated by himself. He was actually a very low level system administrator with an important job of moving information from the continental United States to servers in Hawaii. In doing that, he took data from those servers.

We came up with 42 different series of things that could be done. We shared those actually with the rest of the Government, with industry—the ones that we could—on how to stop insider attacks.

It is interesting. When I talk to most of the financial institutions, more than 50 percent of their concerns come from insider attacks. So these are things that are going on. You have got to do both, and it is all in the behavioral analytics and modeling that would go on to stop that.

So I think we did a good step, but you note a very important point. We were caught flat-footed on Snowden.

Senator MANCHIN. Do you think those steps have been taken to shore that up so that it does not happen again within the NSA? You are not sure if other private organizations have taken your all's advice or lead?

General ALEXANDER. Well, for sure in the NSA because we ran tests. We actually gamed, and then we ran backward data and found that we detected them every time.

Senator MANCHIN. How damaging was the information that he has shared or basically stolen and taken with him and distributed around the world?

General ALEXANDER. I think it was hugely damaging. You can see what the DNI recently said about support to our troops in Afghanistan, the fact that some of that information has gotten out, and our ability to now detect adversaries in Afghanistan has been impacted.

The same thing on terrorist attacks. It has set us back. I personally believe that what he is doing with Russia is hurting our country.

Senator MANCHIN. Do you believe that Snowden should be treated as a traitor?

General ALEXANDER. I do.

Senator MANCHIN. Tried as such.

General ALEXANDER. Yes, I do.

Senator MANCHIN. Thank you.

Chairman McCAIN. Senator Sessions?

Senator SESSIONS. Thank you, Senator McCain, for your leadership and for the series of hearings we have been having.

I would just join with you in your comments about our breaches and Snowden and those issues, General Alexander. I think it is very important. I do not sense from my study of it that we are having any significant threat to individual Americans' liberty. Apparently the President knows everybody that owns a gun in the last campaign and ran ads targeting everybody for every little thing that they favored, they knew about and targeted their campaign message. So we do not have anything like that with regard to our defense analysis.

Well, several years ago, my subcommittee, the Strategic, talked about the threats we might have to our missile and space systems, and we asked that we have reports and analysis of that. Senator Levin, who chaired the committee at the time, and Senator McCain and others agreed that this was not only a problem for our missile systems but for our entire defense systems. I think Dr. Singer just said that earlier.

So we have got legislation, General Alexander, that focuses on that that calls for an analysis of our vulnerabilities and puts now $200 million toward identifying those and creating a response and a plan to protect our vulnerabilities. So I will ask you and Mr. Clark about that, others if you would like to share thoughts about it.

So, first of all, are you familiar with the legislation? Do you think it is a step in the right direction? Do we need to go further? Are we vulnerable and can we take actions that would improve that to limit our vulnerability?

General ALEXANDER. I am not 100 percent steeped in it but I am aware of it, and let me give you my thoughts, if I could.

I think on the vulnerabilities and where we are going to detect and repair those vulnerabilities, that we have got to continue to upgrade how we do that. Let me give you an example. When I had Cyber Command, the issue that we faced was 15,000 enclaves. How do you see all those enclaves? The answer is as the commander responsible for defending our networks, I could not. So when I so how do I know these guys are fixing the vulnerabilities and doing everything we told them to do, well, they report up and so it cascades up. So simple fix is done at manual speed. It takes months when it should be automated. The humans should be out of the loop.

So I think it is a step in the right direction. I would look at and encourage you to look at how we could now automate parts of this because I think it is crucial to blocking those attacks. So I think what you are doing is right. I think there are some steps now that we could take to go beyond that, and I would be happy to talk with some of your people on that.

Senator SESSIONS. Thank you very much.

Mr. Clark? By the way, Mr. Clark, I see you had the distinction of serving on the nuclear submarine Alabama. It is kind of special to me. Tell Senator McCain what you say when you finish off on your announcements on the Alabama?

Mr. CLARK. Roll tide.

[Laughter.]

Chairman McCAIN. It is deeply moving.

Mr. CLARK. It is, is it not?

[Laughter.]

Mr. CLARK. So I would say I agree with the General, obviously, that we need to move towards using automation to a much greater degree to protect our systems from cyber attack. Then also this idea that we need to modernize our networks that deal with missile defense and for strategic deterrence in particular to reduce the number of separate systems involved and reduce the amount of surface area, if you will. So every separate enclave that he described has its own vulnerability to attack like a bunch of little forts that are out there and you have to defend every fort individually. So instead, we need to start bringing more of those into the same enclave so we only have to defend one perimeter as opposed to hundreds of perimeters.

Today in some of these areas where we have had legacy systems cobbled together over time, we have got a bunch of different systems that are now interconnected as opposed to having one system that is able to protect itself automatically. Then that goes back to the automation idea.

I would say a couple other things with regard to our vulnerability in space, though. We also have to deal with the fact that in space, the advent of the new technologies like micro-satellites and servicing robots, to use that again with quotes, but the idea that there are countries that are developing satellites that are small, satellites designed to repair or service or put new batteries into other satellites could also be used to attack a satellite without generating the kind of debris that we would normally assume would deter somebody from attacking a satellite in space. So new technologies that would allow attacks in space are something we have got to consider as well in terms of how do we protect our satellite infrastructure that we depend on for strategic deterrence and for missile defense.

Senator SESSIONS. Thank you.

Mr. Scharre or Dr. Singer, would you like to add to that?

Mr. SCHARRE. Thank you, sir. I would just add on the space side that an important component of enhancing our resiliency in space is off-space backups and networks for redundancy and in part to protect our assets but also to reduce the incentives for attacking them in space. The Department of Defense has had a program to build an aerial layer, the joint aerial layer network, to do communications and position navigation and timing for a number of years that is consistently underfunded and in large part because it is the kind of thing that does not sort of strike a core constituency within the services. So that is something also to add to thinking about our strategic resiliency.

Senator SESSIONS. Dr. Singer?

Dr. SINGER. Thank you, Senator.

I would add a note of caution, maybe a little bit of disagreement on the panel, and then some suggestions.

The note of caution is we should not lean too much on the Cold War parallels of deterrence and mutuality of response, thinking that showing our ability to hit back will deliver 100 percent security in either space and also the idea of the quick timeline. Yes, cyber moves at digital speed, but for example, attacks take not days but months, sometimes years to put together. On average, it is a time period of 205 days between when an attack starts and when the victim finds out about it. In turn, your best response often in cyber attack is not to try and hit back within that 30-minute window with nuclear weapons of the parallel, but in fact, it may be to pause, study it, steer them into areas that they cannot cause harm. So the parallels sometimes are not exact.

The deterrence model that I hope we look for—and we have heard it from the panel here in both space and cyberspace—is more on deterrence by denial, which is building up resilience, whether it is in space by moving from a billion-dollar, single points of failure that can be easily taken out to networks of smaller, cheaper, microsatellites. The same thing in cyberspace, building up resilience in both the military and on the civilian sector.

Within that, I hope we are willing to look at alternative approaches and stop trying to take new capabilities and problems and put them into old boxes. So, for example, I would contrast our defense approach and the way it has not done a great job of pulling in civilian talent. Estonia was mentioned as a model of a victim, one of the first victims of state-level cyber attack, but they have also built up a level of national resilience that we do not have. I would suggest the model of the Estonian Cyber Defense League as an alternative to our approach right now that might be a very positive one.

Thank you.

Senator SESSIONS. Thank you, Mr. Chairman.

Chairman McCAIN. One of the problems with the Estonian model is the privacy issue that causes many of the industries here and companies to be resistant to that model.

Senator Shaheen?

Senator SHAHEEN. Thank you, Mr. Chairman.

Thank you all for testifying this morning.

If I could ask each of you to give a very brief response to do you think the biggest threat as we look at cyber attacks and other challenges to our power grid and to the United States come from the great powers, the great power competition that you referred to, Mr. Clark, or do they come from terrorist groups and non-nation states? General Alexander?

General ALEXANDER. I think the greatest concern comes from nation states. The most frequent attacks come from hackers, terrorists, and others.

Senator SHAHEEN. Mr. Clark?

Mr. CLARK. I agree. I think the greatest threat is going to be from nation states.

Senator SHAHEEN. Does anybody disagree?

Mr. SCHARRE. Yes. I guess I would disagree. I mean, I think in terms of large scale, certainly nation states can bring more power to bear, but I think that this issue of frequency and likelihood is absolutely critical. It is something we need to factor into thinking about threats. I think it is clear that non-state actors can wreak quite a big of destruction on the United States. Deterrence is less effective.

Senator SHAHEEN. General Alexander, I think I understood you to say that we could stop attacks from Iran, Russia, and China, and you prefaced that by talking about the importance of the private sector and their willingness to invest in their own cybersecurity. If we can do that, what has been the impediment to doing that, and how should the operation be organized?

General ALEXANDER. So I think there are several impediments. First, having the right cyber technology, a holistic and comprehensive approach that allows a commercial entity or company to understand when they are being attacked or exploited, the ability to share that information, both from cyber legislation and from a technical perspective, the ability for the Government to receive and then to respond. I do think it is here where the wargaming and other things would go on. So what is your response going to be if these events occur? So you have thought that through ahead of time and you know how and what and the commands know what they are going to do.

Senator SHAHEEN. Well, again, if we can do that, should it be organized under the Cyber Command within DOD or should it be organized someplace else? Why have we not done that already?

General ALEXANDER. Well, this goes back to the organizational structure that was asked previously. We have parts of this in DHS that is really responsible for the resiliency, correctly. We have the DOD defend the Nation. Then you have the Department of Justice with the responsibility for criminal activities.

What Secretary Gates said is you have got those three, but they are all talking about the same domain and you can go very quickly from, as Mr. Scharre brought up, a non-nation state actor acting like a nation state actor.

So I think you have to have war games and we have to go through that. We have not organized ourselves right, nor did we bring Government and industry together and we do not have the legislation to allow that to occur.

Senator SHAHEEN. Are you suggesting that we should organize it within the Department of Defense?

General ALEXANDER. I think the Department of Defense has to have a key if not the lead role because when push comes to shove and somebody has to respond for the good of the Nation, it is the Defense Department. If our Nation is under attack, they are the ones that are going to be held accountable.

Senator SHAHEEN. Thank you.

Mr. Scharre, you recently wrote about the dangers of radical transparency and how our adversaries would be able to exploit what our military does because they will be able to get that information because of our transparency. Can you explain or suggest what we might do to respond to that?

Mr. SCHARRE. Sure. So I think there are a couple of components of that. One is the digitization of Government data. Certainly we have seen this with incidents like Snowden and Bradley Manning and the ability to take large amounts of data. Now, there are obviously a number of efforts underway inside the Government.

But I think there is also an element of transparency in terms of our military operations being conducted. We have seen this transformed domestic policing in the United States. Now this era of ubiquitous smart phones where every action can be recorded. I worry that our forces on the ground are not adequately trained and prepared for that. We have seen one-off incidents in these wars where there is an incident like Koran burning or someone urinating on corpses and their strategic effects. But a world where every action by one of our soldiers and marines on the ground is recorded and tweeted around in real time is something that I do not think we are prepared for. I say this in large part from personal experience fighting as an NCO on the ground in Iraq and Afghanistan where occasionally we will have interactions with the population where things are rough. These are difficult conflicts. But having it go viral is a very different kind of environment.

Senator SHAHEEN. My time is up. But, Mr. Chairman, if I could ask just one more question.

Secretary Gates, when he was here, referenced the fact that the U.S. Information Agency is defunct now and that our strategic efforts to communicate really pale in comparison to some of our adversaries. Certainly that is true with Russia. It is true with ISIS I think. So how do any of you suggest that we better respond to that, and should those efforts to get out, given the challenges of transparency that you mentioned, but our need to do a better job in these areas—how do we do that and who should head that effort? Should it be Defense? Should it be the State Department? Mr. Scharre, since you are answering.

Mr. SCHARRE. Yes. I think it is worth exploring the idea of a new agency. It is possible. That is a good solution. It is possible that does not help. But certainly we do need to adapt our communications to this digital and social media age.

Mr. CLARK. I would add that I think one area that we have not fully exploited since the Cold War is taking advantage of the demonstration of new technologies, whether they are successful or not, and communicating that to potential adversaries to create uncertainty in their mind as to whether they are going to be successful. So we develop a new railgun. We develop a new laser. We develop an electronic warfare system that we think is going to offer a lot of promise. Or we go build a few of them and go demonstrate them and then communicate that so that it is more widely understood. So I think we could take a radical transparency and turn around and use it for our own purposes by creating uncertainty in the minds of potential enemies.

Senator SHAHEEN. I certainly agree with that.

Dr. Singer?

Dr. SINGER. Part of why they have been so successful at is they are using a technology that is inherently networked and coming at it with a network-style approach. So I would guard against us coming at it with a kind of 1940's centralized approach. That is part of why we are not doing well.

Second is they know specifically what they want to do. We have not yet figured out whether we want to counter-narrative or take them off the network or, in turn, take advantage of this very same radical transparency and intelligence gather on them. So on one hand, ISIL is getting its message out. On the other hand, we are gathering more information about them than any adversary before because of this. So we need to figure that out for ourselves.

Then third, why they have been able to do it in some manners better than us is that they have cohesion between their communication strategy and their battlefield operations. So, for example, before they launched the operation against Mosul, they had preset hash tags ready to go. We do not have that kind of cohesion between our strategic communications and our battlefield operations.

Senator SHAHEEN. Thank you all.

Thank you, Mr. Chairman.

Chairman MCCAIN. Senator Fischer?

Senator FISCHER. Thank you, Mr. Chairman.

Dr. Singer, earlier you said the per-unit cost of the cart is driving where we steer the horse. I would like to open it up to the entire panel and ask what can we do about cutting. Where can we do less? A lot of times we talk about where we can do more. I would like your opinions on where we can do less with research, with buying, training. What will we not need in the future? Dr. Singer?

Dr. SINGER. I think you have heard from the panel many great ideas, and the question is whether we will be able to implement them in shifts in everything from our personnel system and professional military education, all the way to the example of distinguishing between the type of systems and the requirements that we build for them when we approach it, the problem of legacy systems.

Another thing that I would put specifically on the table is our tendency to plan and assume for the best and then we act surprised when things do not work out that way. That was what I was referencing in terms of the Pontiac Aztek of war problem where we have systems—and again, all of you are thinking about certain systems in terms of we develop a warship that our Navy's own tester says will not be survivable in combat, and then we act surprised and say, gosh, we got to fix that, or tanker aircraft that are planned not to be in anything above a medium threat environment. Then, of course, the enemy gets a vote, and we go, gosh, we should have figured out about that.

What I am getting as that we too often, in an attempt to—again, we get caught within this dynamic of the per-unit costs. It is shaping everything from what we develop to, oh, my goodness, we cannot change the amount we were planning to buy for what it will do to the future per-unit cost of it. As part of this, we should also be able—and I would associate myself with the other remarks—revisualize how certain weapons systems can take on new and important roles the way the B-52 bomber, for example, went from strategic nuclear deterrence operations to close air support. We may be able to rethink that approach in everything from what is an aircraft carrier—will submarines be able to take on that role—to the long-range strike bomber. Is it just for strike, or will it be able to take on ISR or even air-to-air combat roles in the future? These are possibilities if we allow them to happen and not be locked in by past decisions.

Senator FISCHER. Mr. Scharre?

Mr. SCHARRE. Thank you, Senator.

I think there is an issue of quantity. There certainly are places to trim the quantities of assets, not just to have fewer numbers of more capable things but then to trade that for larger numbers of lower-cost systems. So moving to this issue of thinking about, as Dr. Singer mentioned, sort of the major combat assets as—think of them as sort of a quarterback behind a fight, a bomber that is not just carrying assets to the fight, but the pilots are controlling a swarm of maybe lower-cost unmanned vehicles and a submarine as the hub of a network of autonomous undersea vehicles or undersea payloads that then expand the capabilities we actually have in the fight.

Mr. CLARK. What this kind of points to is separating the platform, if you will, from the payload. So what we have done in the past is we have developed the ship or aircraft with all of its systems built into it, and we would then periodically modernize that by tearing it all apart and then rebuilding it all with new technology every 10 or 20 years or so. We need to move towards not buying the next generation of these aircraft and ships and other platforms in a way that integrates all those systems, but instead buy much cheaper and less equipped things and then equip them with payloads that can then adapt much more quickly over time because the innovation cycle for something like a missile or a radar system or a passive radar sensor is much quicker than that of the overall platform. So we can afford to go to cheaper platforms.

So in terms of what we have today, I would not say that we want to throw stuff on the scrap heap that we currently have in the fleet, but we want to look at ways we can reequip it with the next generation of payloads. Instead of replacing them with another highly integrated airplane or ship, let us keep them, take out their old stuff, and just use then interchangeable payloads in the future to start reducing the cost of these platforms in the future. So to get to the F-35 example, so maybe the F-35 is the last aircraft we buy that is really a purpose-built strike fighter. To Dr. Singer's point, maybe you do end up with airplanes in the future that are just larger and have bigger sensors and they do all the missions and the payload changes to accommodate that.

General ALEXANDER. Senator, I think one of the things that we should look at is—the commercial industry spends billions if not trillions of dollars a year in cybersecurity alone. When you think about all that money that is being spent, it is being spent to solve their problem. But they, if they work together, create a sector solution and that sector solution could be very important for defending our country. If we had Government and industry work together in a way that was meaningful so that what they applied those resources for helped give them more reflective surface in cyber—it would tell the Government when the Government has to act—you could focus Government resources where it is really needed.

So I think the idea of having a war game and then looking at how you get the financial sector, the energy sector, the health care sector, and the Government together and maybe a few others, put those in a room and look at what they are doing, what you would find out is, you know, one big bank along is a spending almost $750

million a year in cybersecurity. What if it was done in a way that
helped protect the whole sector, and if they worked together, that
surface would be far better than anything the Government could
do. We need them to do that so that the Government can focus on
what you want, especially the Defense Department, to do.

Senator FISCHER. Mr. Scharre, you were talking about swarms
and a change in warfighting. If I could, Mr. Chairman, we hear
about platforms. We hear about payloads. What about personnel?
Are we going to be looking at the same infantry in 20, 30, 40 years?
The infantry can take and hold ground. Can technology replace
that?

Mr. SCHARRE. Well, I think technology can certainly aid in taking
ground. Yes. When it comes to holding it and then building up a
security infrastructure that can pass on to someone else, that is
something that is going to require interpersonal interaction.

Could we use robotic systems in war to help ground maneuver
warfare? I think absolutely. I think there is a lot of opportunities.
The Army probably is not yet seizing to look at something like a
modern day robotics, the Louisiana maneuvers, to experiment with
maneuver warfare. But when it comes to sitting down with tribal
elders, a person has got to do that.

Senator FISCHER. Thank you.

Thank you, Mr. Chair.

Chairman MCCAIN. Senator Kaine?

Senator KAINE. Thank you, Mr. Chairman.

Thank you to the witnesses.

General Alexander, you talked about and we read about all the
time the number of cyber attacks on the Nation or on governmental
agencies that are occurring with greater frequency. I think you use
350 cyber attacks. I am not sure what unit of time that was. Give
us a good example of a counter cyber attack that the United States
has undertaken. So when we have been attacked, give me a good
example of something we have done in response.

General ALEXANDER. Senator, I cannot give you that in this
forum, but I think that is something that would be good to discuss
for the committee in a classified session.

Senator KAINE. I just want to make this point. I thought that
was going to be your answer.

There is not a deterrence doctrine if people do not know what the
response will be. The President last week said he was going send
50 special forces to Syria. I know to the number how many bombing raids we have run in the war against ISIL that is now in its
nearly 16th month. We know the number of personnel that are
deployed.

When the American public and policymakers read over and over
again in the press about cyber attacks on the Nation, they are very
public. But when we cannot discuss even with the committee in a
public setting or with the American public what we are doing in
response, it kind of leads to a little bit of a feeling of like we are
impotent against these attacks. I know that we are not. But if we
can talk about troop deployments in the war on ISIL and bombing
sorties that are run but we cannot talk in open session about what
we do in response to cyber attacks that are every bit in the public
news as any of the bombing campaigns are, I think it really leads

to a sense of helplessness by the public and the committees themselves. I hope we will have a follow-up and talk about this.

General ALEXANDER. Could I offer, Senator?

Senator KAINE. Please.

General ALEXANDER. Let us go hypothetical instead of actual, and we could talk about hypothetically what the Defense Department could do and others.

Senator KAINE. I would rather actually move to another topic. Hypotheticals are great. Why can we know actual in so many realms of what we do in defense, but we are not willing to talk actual about cyber? Because we certainly hear about the actual attacks on us. So I think that raises a question I would like to explore more.

A very interesting hearing, all your written testimony and oral testimony too. The title was provocative, "the Future of Warfare." A lot of the discussion has been about technical technology issues.

I think one of the interesting areas about the future of warfare is the question of unilateral being with partners. We were attacked on 9/11 by al Qaeda and we immediately assembled a coalition that amounted to about 60 nations to try to respond to that. The first thought after the attack on Pearl Harbor was not we ought to go out and assemble a coalition, although there were other nations, obviously the allied nations that were involved in World War II.

Is there something unique about the future—certainly the current and the future of warfare that renders this whole idea of coalitions kind of more of a common feature? The F-35 is a platform that was built with the participation of nine partner nations, not just different service branches but partner nations. Talk about coalitions and alliances in the future of warfare. I would just be curious to any of your thoughts about that.

General ALEXANDER. If I could, in the cyber realm, we would be much better off with partners in this area. Think about the undersea cables. They come from the United Kingdom to us, 12 of the 17 or 18. So the United Kingdom and Europe—if they had a similar approach to cybersecurity and they agreed to defend their end, we defend our end, we have now moved our defense out to Europe for our country. I think that is a very good thing and we could do things like that in this space. So I do believe there is much need for collaboration, but it also brings in all the issues now you have with civil liberties and privacy because every nation sees it different, even in Europe. Every one of those see it differently. So I think we have got to set the standard, and that is one of the things that we could do as a country.

Mr. CLARK. I would say the benefit that we get from coalitions, though, is primarily non-material. I would argue that they do not bring a lot of necessarily military capabilities to bear that are easily applied in a unified command context. It actually makes it a little bit harder if you are trying to do it with multiple nations' forces. But what they do bring, as General Alexander was saying, is access to areas that we would otherwise not be able to base from or operate from or be able to monitor.

It also provides, if you will, the political top cover so that if we can demonstrate that that is the way that we are used to operating, it may drive our competitors or our adversaries into a calculation where they realize that, well, I am not just going to be upsetting the United States if I take this action, but I will also be upsetting a number of my other neighbors, which could create other problems down the road politically for them. So there may be a political benefit in the long term to us managing things through a coalition.

Chairman MCCAIN. Senator Rounds?

Senator ROUNDS. Thank you, Mr. Chairman.

General Alexander, do we have a stated doctrine with regard to what is a cyber attack or do we have a defined limit where we identify something as an act of war if our defense, our energy, or our financial resources are attacked?

General ALEXANDER. The only thing that I know that comes close to that is the President's statement of 2009 about how we would respond using any form of power, cyber, military, diplomatic, to respond to a cyber. There are no rules of the road or red lines in cyber. I think war games can help tighten some of that up and should.

Senator ROUNDS. Would anyone disagree with that analysis?

Mr. CLARK. I would add one thing, that one of the challenges you have in cyber is that if we try to use a cyber capability to respond to a cyber attack, we may end up making clear to the adversary the access that we have into his networks. So one problem we have is we do not want to burn the source. So if we are attacked in cyberspace, we might need to go to some other means to respond because we do not want to give up the fact that we have got access to his networks and are able then to monitor his activities in the future. As General Alexander said, we might be able to take advantage of the attack to actually gain new access that we do not want to make clear to the enemy.

Senator ROUNDS. Yes. Mr. Singer?

Dr. SINGER. I would just add the key is not the means. It is not that it is cyber. It is the end effect which will determine it. So whether it is through cyber or a missile as to whether it causes loss of life, physical damage, even if someone set a—a foreign adversary set a fire that killed hundreds of Americans, we would not say, gosh, you used matches not cyber or a missile. So cyber can be a little bit of a misdirection. It is more about the end effect and how we judge that.

Senator ROUNDS. Do we need a different doctrine? Do we need an established doctrine to determine whether or not a cyber act is an act of war?

Mr. CLARK. I would say we need to have a real clear definition of what we think constitutes an attack that would be meriting of a response because we do that in the physical realm to a much greater degree. Obviously, this gets built up as a body of action over time. So it is precedent that does it to some extent.

General ALEXANDER. If I could, to answer that question, I think when you look at our NATO responsibilities, I think we do have to have this laid out. What we cannot do is walk into a war because we did not understand that this would be an act of war so that if someone were to attack one of our NATO allies and cause destruction and lives, what constitutes an act of war is not really clearly stated. There has been a lot of stuff in the Tallinn Papers that have been written, but it does not get to the point of this is clear. So I think we need to have those discussions in a classified and unclassified realm so everybody understands. I do agree with it is the intent of the individuals. If their intent is to do harm, I think you now need to look at where you take --

Senator ROUNDS. Would you share with me what you consider to be an appropriate response should there be an act of war in the cyber realm?

General ALEXANDER. I think first ideally you could prevent it, but if you could not prevent it, I think you now have two things that are going on, the resilience in your networks, bringing those back up, and then a whole series of actions from political, economic, diplomatic, military. In cyber, there are a lot of things you could do to stop that nation from communicating outside that nation with other tools. I think it is those types of capabilities and wargaming and things that ought to be looked at analogous to the way we did armored warfare 70 years ago.

Senator ROUNDS. Sometimes we talk about this in a way in which we have a tendency to literally scare ourselves because we are talking about how serious these could be. Do we have the capability and the resources right now to actually respond should we have that type of a cyber attack that would amount to—if we define it properly as an act of war, are we in a position today as a country to respond to an act of war?

General ALEXANDER. We have 40 offensive teams that were created at U.S. Cyber Command. Those teams have some great capabilities. It does not cover the whole world, but it gives you a great starting point. I think our first thought in 2010 was let us set up with the initial force structure that we needed it, set it up in terms of offense and defense in teams that could actually do offensive actions to defend the country.

Senator ROUNDS. Anyone have anything to add to that? Yes, sir. Dr. Singer?

Dr. SINGER. I would just add two things. The first is the idea of assuming that our response would have to be limited just to cyber means. If someone carries out an act of war against us using cyber means, we are not and should not be limited in our response to use other means. That is why we are seeing that kind of deterrence hold.

The second, though, is to—as General Alexander said, we have built up great cyber offense capability. There are many things that Mr. Snowden did, but one of the other things he did is revealed that we have very potent cyber offense capability. I would add, though, to those who believe that building up more will deliver deterrence, the question why has that not delivered deterrence yet. There is no question that we have great cyber offense capability and yet the attacks have continued to come. That is why I echo back to we need to do more about building up deterrence through denial which is making ourselves more resilient both in military and civilian means so we can shrug off those attacks, which therefore makes the attacks less productive, less likely on us.

Senator ROUNDS. Thank you, Mr. Chairman.

Chairman MCCAIN. Senator King?

Senator KING. Thank you, Mr. Chairman.

Dr. Singer, I must compliment you. To found a technology advisory firm called NeoLuddite is an act of genius.

I also enjoyed your Churchill quote. One of my favorite Churchill quotes was he was once asked how he thought history would treat his role in World War II. His response was, "very well because I intend to write it."

On this issue of deterrence—and I think Senator Rounds really hit the point, and I think we should follow up on this. It is the question of what is an act of war and when will we respond because if an act of war is not defined, your opponent has to know that you are going to consider it an act of war and that there will be a response. Mr. Singer, I think your point is well taken, that it does not necessarily have to be a cyber response. But I do think there does need to be some response. Deterrence by denial, it seems to me—ultimately you have got to have some offensive capability. You have got to be able to punch back or you are simply always on the defensive. You are nodding your head. I assume you agree with that concept.

Dr. SINGER. I very much agree. I will compliment you in turn. Thank you for your kind words.

I have an article coming out next week on this question of deterrence and the three approaches are what the committees wrestled with. It is one to set very clear norms so both sides or all the sides understand what is and is not an act of war so that there is no miscalculation.

The second is to understand that you can respond, but you can respond in many other means, many other areas and it is not just through military. It may be through trade. It may be through espionage, whatever. There was a far more complex game going on in the Cold War where your only response was you hit me with a nuke. I threaten to hit you back.

Then the third is this point about deterrence by denial, something that was not possible in the Cold War. The idea of civilian involvement was kind of—you know, the bomb shelters and the like were not very useful. Deterrence by denial, though, now would be an incredible useful concept, and importantly, resilience works not just against state-level attacks, but it is also effective against all the other attacks out there, whether it is non-state actors like terrorists or just criminal groups.

Senator KING. On that point, General, good to see you again. I think a point you made that I had not really thought about was the idea of a joint private sector cybersecurity effort perhaps facilitated by the Government but not with Government involvement so we do not have the privacy issues. But it strikes me as inefficient in the extreme to have Bank of America spending billions on cybersecurity and Anthem and Target and Walmart when, in reality, they are all chasing the same problem. It may be that a consortium—as I recall, there was a semiconductor consortium some years ago—to deal with this in a joint way might save the private sector a lot of money. The Government could just act as a facilitator.

Dr. Clark, I think an important point that has been made today—and it was made in one of the hearings the other day—was instead of building weapons systems that have absolutely everything that are going to last 40 years and therefore, by definition, be obsolete, we ought to building modular systems, if you will, that can be modernized on the fly rather than starting all over again. Is that essentially what your testimony was?

Mr. CLARK. Yes, definitely. That gives you the ability to take advantage of the technology refresh cycle that exists for those smaller systems. We talked about Moore's Law and how that results in a doubling of computer programming power every 12 to 18 months. The computer is really the heart of almost every one of our payloads, whether it is a sensor or a missile or even a smart bomb today, or unmanned vehicle. So we should take advantage of the fact that that technology refresh cycle is going to be so fast and develop those payloads on a much faster timeline.

Senator KING. Trying to develop a weapon system that has everything for everybody at one time that will be fixed in time is just the wrong way to go.

Mr. CLARK. Which gets back to the requirements problem. If I define my requirements in isolation from what the technology might be able to give me in a near-term time frame, I end up aspiring to something I will never be able to achieve.

Senator KING. The requirements proliferate because everybody wants their—it is the problem of a camel is a horse designed by a committee.

Mr. CLARK. Right, instead of defining requirements in conjunction with what your technology is already delivering.

Senator KING. Dr. Singer, if your article has not gone to press, I would urge a quote from Robert Frost, good fences make good neighbors. When people know what the rules are, that is when you can avoid conflict.

A final question just for the record. General Alexander, very chilling in your early testimony that we will not have time for human decision-making in responding to some of these kinds of attacks. In other words, the 30 minutes or an hour for the missiles is now in a matter of seconds. The question is how do we war-game and prepare a response that can be done instantaneously without the intervention of human discretion. I think that is an issue—my time has expired, but I think that is an issue that deserves some serious thought and discussion.

Thank you, gentlemen, very much. This has been very illuminating.

[The information referred to follows:]

To answer this question, I think it is important to look at our offensive and defensive capabilities, at a classified level, and see what we are capable of doing. With those insights, you immediately come to the conclusion that some of our responses could be pre-programmed, to operate at network speed, consistent with policies set by the Commander-in-Chief, in consultation with Congress and the military leadership, as appropriate. This requires a detailed set of analyses about the options available to our civilian and military leadership, and the Rules of Engagement the Administration would give to USCYBERCOM [Cyber Command] to conduct, essentially, defensive measures to protect our Nation. Some of these options we discussed with Secretary Carter, when he was the DEPSECDEF [Deputy Secretary of Defense]. It is my professional opinion that Congress and the Administration should be in sync with the ROE [Rules of Engagement] given to USCYBERCOM in these cases.

To evolve these ROE, I believe we should conduct a series of wargames to fully understand the issues and measures that should be implemented.

When we walk through these wargames, I think we are likely to come to the conclusion that USCYBERCOM and NSA have to have network speed access to detect threats and respond to attacks on our Nation.

Because any delay in responding to cyber attacks could have catastrophic results, it is critical that we think through these issues now, as a nation, and that all elements of our political, civilian, and military leaders—from Congress to the White House and the Pentagon—be on the same page about how to respond to these threats.

Chairman McCAIN. Dr. Singer, I would suggest words of Chairman Mao. It is always darkest before it is totally black.

[Laughter.]

Chairman McCAIN. Senator Ernst?

Senator ERNST. Thank you, Mr. Chair.

Gentlemen, thank you for your support to our Nation in so many varying ways. I think the discussion today has been very beneficial I think for all of us and our constituencies.

General Alexander, I would like to start with you, sir. We have spent a lot of time talking about the cyber threats that exist out there and the devastating effects to our networks, should they be attacked or when they are attacked, and really the ability to recruit and retain some talent to deal with the cutting-edge threats that exist out there.

What I would like to know is a little bit more. How can we utilize our Reserve and our National Guard forces to bring in some of the best and the brightest? We have a lot of folks that certainly serve in very similar capacities in their civilian employment. Is there a way that we can use them to leverage our forces?

General ALEXANDER. Actually, Senator, that is a great question. We were doing that when I was on. I know that continues. So each of the National Guard units are setting up cyber teams that would also help. As you note, some of these have some of the best technical experts in civilian industry that partner with us. So you go out to the State of Washington with Microsoft employees or all around the world—all around the U.S. I think there are some great partnerships there, and it also gives you an opportunity to bring those on to active duty when you need them and then taking them off.

Finally, if we work it right, it also helps provide security for the State and local government.

Senator ERNST. I think that is wonderful. I know that in my transportation company, we had some computer whizzes working in the civilian industry. They were truck drivers when we were mobilized. But a lot of talent that exists out there.

Mr. Scharre, Paul, I know that we have spent some time talking about future personnel generations in our Department of Defense. I would like to visit a little bit with you about, again, the National Guard and the Reserves and where you see their role in the future, whether it is Army, Navy, Air Force, Marines, and how they can support future conflicts.

Mr. SCHARRE. Thanks, Senator.

I think this issue of civilian expertise is a unique capability that the National Guard and Reserve brings to the table. Your example of computer experts driving trucks—and I saw active duty reservists—many similar things in Iraq—were even doing civil affairs functions. We still had people misaligned. We are not as aligned as well as maybe they could be with some of these skills that actually are resident in a Guard and Reserve force. So a process inside the Department to actually identify—have service members self-identify those skills and allow them to be tracked inside the Department so that if the Nation needs to be able to draw upon that, we could know who are these experts would be extremely valuable and I think a way to really increase even further the skills and capabilities that the National Guard and Reserve bring to the table.

Senator ERNST. I think that is a great idea. I know that we do identify many of our civilian skill sets through the Guard and Reserves, but I do not know that the DOD truly pays attention to that. I think we have a lot of, as I said, talent and abilities that could be better utilized on or with an active duty force.

Do you think that the DOD will continue to rely heavily upon our Guard and Reserves as we move into future conflicts in outlying years as heavily as they have maybe in the past 14 years?

Mr. SCHARRE. I think there is no question they will continue to play a valuable role. Certainly we have asked a lot of Guard and Reserve members, and they have given a lot in the last 14 years. So I think they will continue to be a valuable contributor in the future.

Senator ERNST. Thank you.

I will move on to a different topic and, Mr. Clark, maybe you can assist with this. Today I did lead a number of my colleagues in a letter regarding our concern for Russia's activities near some of our underwater cables. It is very concerning because these are fiber optic cables and they carry everything from sensitive information, communications, many of these things that are vital to our economic stability. I know that it is a very sensitive topic, but I think it is pretty vital that we start talking about our interests in underwater fiber optic cables.

So are you concerned at all about the security that we have that either exists or does not exist out there? If you could expound on that, please.

Mr. CLARK. I am very concerned about it. Those cables carry trillions of dollars in financial transactions every year. About 90 percent of the world's economy runs on undersea cables as a result of that.

The Russians for a long time have had an undersea reconnaissance program where they go and look at things under the water, and they have taken an interest recently in undersea cables. We can tell by the areas where they are operating that they are looking for something down there in the vicinity of undersea cables.

Out in the open ocean, these undersea cables are fairly hard to find because you kind of have to search a large area. But in the areas where they have their landings on the shore, either the United States, over in Europe, or in the Middle East, they are relatively easy to locate and then trace back into the water.

I think one concern we would have is in conflict. Those cables could be easily broken. They are broken fairly regularly today as a result of trawlers or anchors that take them up. Today the responsibility for responding or replacing or repairing those cables lies with industry. So they have on call the cable laying ships that go out and fix them. But you are talking about time frames of weeks to months to repair a cable that has been damaged as a result of either hostile or accidental action.

So one concern I would have is we need to improve the ability to rapidly respond to these kinds of attacks to be able to restore the activity on those cables. Then two, we need to have better monitoring capabilities in the vicinity of these landings where it is a target-rich environment for an undersea vehicle or a ship that is going to deploy a remotely operated vehicle to go attack them.

But there are technologies out there that could provide the ability to monitor these areas pretty well, but counter-UAV [Unmanned Aerial Vehicle] technology will be a key part of it and being able to find something small like Dr. Singer and Mr. Scharre have talked about is going to be really hard. So we need to come up with better capabilities to detect these very small underwater vehicles that could be used against undersea cables. But it is a huge potential vulnerability that could be exploited both in peacetime or in war.

Senator ERNST. Yes, I agree. Thank you very much. I appreciate that. I think that that is something that we need to turn our direction to also.

So thank you, Mr. Chair.

Chairman MCCAIN. Senator Hirono?

Senator HIRONO. Thank you, Mr. Chairman and to all of you who are testifying.

The Defense Department has used a technology, basically quality over quantity, to stay ahead of the other countries. So one of the other hearings we had said that we are falling behind in our ability to rely on our technical superiority. So do you share that view, and if so, what are some very fundamental steps we should be taking in order to increase our capacity, technological capacity? Any of you can answer.

Mr. SCHARRE. I will start.

I think one of the main factors is time. How do we shorten the time by which we develop major programs? Mr. Clark talked about modularity, thinking about payloads over platforms. I would also encourage us to think about software over payloads. You can upgrade software very rapidly. But there are even some more sort of fundamental shifts that people are thinking about. You know, this DARPA program that I mentioned earlier SoSITE [System of Systems Integration Technology, Experimentation], is thinking about basically taking a major platform and breaking it apart entirely into a larger number of basically just the payloads that are all interacting together, and that is something worth experimenting with and exploring.

Senator HIRONO. So are you saying that we should spend more money on R&D or is it also the way we are structuring how the money is spent?

Mr. SCHARRE. I think the way in which you spend the money is absolutely critical.

Senator HIRONO. How would you change how we are spending our money?

Mr. SCHARRE. The R&D spending in the Department is very decentralized and fragmented. So just a more centralized process that focuses, as Mr. Clark mentioned, on the key areas, and this effort is underway with the LRDP [Long Range Development Plan], long-range something something defense acronym—you know, I think are beneficial in that regard.

Dr. SINGER. Senator, I would just add. I think it is both the way, but we also clearly do not spend enough on R&D. We have seen the percentages go down both on the Government side but also as a Nation, as was mentioned, in the defense industry side as well. The issue of quantity/quality is not just in terms of the weapon system but just simply if you run out of missiles, say, for example, in a fight, you will have to exit. So you may survive but you have deferred to the enemy in that time.

Senator HIRONO. Did you want to——

Mr. CLARK. I would just add one more thing is that we have a pretty good investment inside DOD in R&D. It is not well focused, as we talked about.

In addition to that, industry used to do a lot of internal research and development with their own money to go explore new military capabilities that might be beneficial in the future. They have reduced that investment significantly with the reduction over the last several years in the amount of procurement because it is normally a percentage of procurement. Also there are some things that the Department is doing that has been disincentivizing industry from pursuing its own internal research and development that has in the past given us things like stealth and things like new radar technology. So I think one thing we ought to look at is how do we encourage industry to be independently looking at problems that they could address with their new technologies.

Senator HIRONO. Perhaps one of the ways that we incentivize the private sector is, of course, to have the potential of technology transfer in whatever research that they are doing and developing.

For Mr. Scharre and Mr. Clark, what impacts do you anticipate our reliance on fossil fuels will have on our planning and the effectiveness of our future warfighters? What is your assessment of the Department's progress in terms of reducing its reliance on fossil fuel sources?

Mr. SCHARRE. I think there are a couple key reasons to do so. One is, of course, strategic risk and vulnerability. Another one is cost. But an important one is alternative energy solutions can help increase the endurance for many various sort of long-endurance capabilities, particularly robotics, that we could put out on the battlefield. So things like better batteries, fuel cells, solar power can allow us to put persistent surveillance sensors out there to help detect the enemy for a very long period of time, months or years at a time. So there are some significant operational advantages as well.

Mr. CLARK. It is about not so much fossil fuels as just reducing our energy dependence in general because what you see is we have to project forces over a very long distance because all of our friends and allies are an ocean away from us. So we are generally transferring those forces over a long distance, and even when they get there, they are having to operate at the very edge of our logistics chain. So reducing the amount of energy they need in general would be important. Taking advantage of technologies that do not require fuel at all would be important. So the idea of going to new battery technologies that are able to last for a very long period time and then eventually be recharged by the sun or by returning to some docking station would be a very good way for us to reduce the tether that we have to maintain because right now we have to have refueling aircraft and ships out at the edge with the ships that they are refueling and then refuel a ship, for example, every few days while it is operating, and then aircraft, obviously, have to operate for a much shorter period of time before they need to be refueled. So moving to energy technologies that do not require fuel to be delivered to the platform on a regular basis I think would be very important.

Senator HIRONO. Thank you.

Chairman MCCAIN. Senator Sullivan?

Senator SULLIVAN. Thank you, Mr. Chair.

Sorry Senator Hirono and I had to step out for a few minutes. We were actually celebrating the 240th birthday of the United States Marine Corps. So we had to welcome the chair and ranking member as members of the Navy and the Army.

Chairman MCCAIN. A dark day.

[Laughter.]

Senator SULLIVAN. Gentlemen, thanks very much for your testimony.

General Alexander, I was actually struck by your testimony in one area that—well, in a couple areas I thought it was very insightful. But one of the things that we have been hearing about in terms of cyber is this idea that—this notion that we are constantly being attacked, we are constantly—and you mentioned it. Some of the dollars and statistics you have in your testimony on cyber crime and what that costs is really eye-popping.

But there has been this notion of us being on defense, defense, defense. One thing that I liked about your testimony is that you talked about a little in terms of offense where we have invented a lot of this technology. We are the leader in it still. So there are all kinds of opportunities for offense.

Could you just provide some examples of that? I mean, the chairman's opening statement about turning technologies into offensive advantages I think was very illuminating from a historical perspective. But what are some opportunities in terms of offense that we have with regard to cyber?

General ALEXANDER. Well, there are a number of offensive capabilities. I think first and foremost you have to be able to see what the adversary is doing, hence the need for the commercial sector to be part of the solution so what is hitting them can be seen by everyone. So if you think about how two computers actually talk— you know, I want to talk to you. You come back and say on this channel. We go to the ACK [Acknowledged] and NAK [Not Acknowledged] kind of thing. That takes time, milliseconds. If you think about some computer trying to get in while that is happening, if the Government can see it, the Government can stop it or at least delay it or stop the router or do things with it. So what you have is opportunities to change what is happening in cyberspace with offensive tools that would defend the country.

The issue comes down to so what would you authorize, for example, Cyber Command to do in order to defend it. You might say, well, I am going to let you do everything you can to block all the way to where it is originating from, but I do not want you to destroy systems yet. Destroying systems is going to go a step further. But technically speaking—and you have seen this—you could destroy a computer in cyberspace by getting on it and doing certain things to it. So the technical ability is there. It is public record. Now all you need is access, and how you get into that access is where you take the capabilities of an NSA with a Cyber Command and FBI at times and put those together. So you have tremendous opportunities.

I think when we look back at our capability, you look at we are the most integrated networked society in the world. We look back, and we say look at all these opportunities in the offense, and then you look at ours on the defense. You would say, man, we are broke. If we throw rocks, we have all these glass windows. First step, fix those.

Senator SULLIVAN. Let me ask just kind of a related question on—I know there has been a lot of discussion in this testimony on deterrence or raising the costs of cyber attacks. It seems to me—and I would welcome any of your opinions—that if you are from an authoritarian regime like Russia or Iran or China, they in some ways have an advantage because they can just deny and lie. No, we had nothing to do with that, even though they did or they do.

But you mentioned like one example to me that the Iranians were attacking our financial system. Would it make sense for us to say publicly that if you do that again, we will crash your entire financial sector? Is that the kind of thing that we should be looking at in terms of raising the cost? Because it seems to me if you are an authoritarian regime, you can lie about who is doing it, that the costs of actually all these attacks is almost minimal because we do not react. Should we maybe look at being a little more public in upping the ante and saying if you do this, North Korea, Iran, China, we will respond? In some of these countries, I am sure we could crash their whole economy. What would be a problem with that kind of deterrence that makes it a little more transparent but raises the cost dramatically? Then, of course, if we announce that, we would have to act. I am curious. Any of the panelists, what would you think of something a little more transparent from our perspective, and do we have a disadvantage when we are dealing with authoritarian regimes that routinely lie about this issue?

Mr. CLARK. I would say one thing we have to think about is the fact that the deterrent action might need to be fairly proportional with the action it is intended to deter because it will not have credibility otherwise. If we say that because the Iranians are attacking some of our banking sector, that we would go and crash their financial system, that might be disproportional, and therefore they do not find that to be a credible threat because they will say, well, they will never do that.

Senator SULLIVAN. But what if we did it?

Mr. CLARK. Well, if we did it, it may deter further action, but it may be seen by the international community as being highly disproportionate. So we might need to come up with a more proportional reaction to things like that so that the adversary will say, well, he actually could do that. I mean, this is something that the United States could do in response.

That gets to where maybe the response needs to be not in cyberspace but in another domain, for example, electronic warfare, jamming, small attacks on oil infrastructure. Those could all be undertaken with a relatively small amount of collateral effects while also demonstrating the resolve of the United States and being able to do something that they would find to be credible and that we could repeat but that does not cause such a huge damaging reaction that people are not going to believe we will ever use it.

Dr. SINGER. Senator, the challenge in this is there is not the mutual, in terms of the old mutual shared destruction. So, for example, we are far more vulnerable to cyber attack than North Korea, but that is actually a good thing because we are integrated with the global economy. We have freedom. We have all these other things. We would not want to be in that position that they are in. So recognizing the lack of mutuality, echoing the points about maybe looking at other deterrence angles.

But I would add one more important thing. When we are talking about offense, when we are talking about steering Cyber Command to taking on these roles and the civilian lead, it is moving it and us away from its role in clear warfare itself, and the determinant of success or failure in future wars with cyber will not be thinking about it individually but will be how it is integrated with other warfighting capacity. So the more we focus on the power grid, the less it is integrating that cyber capability in terms of war, using it to take down an air defense so it is cohesive with your warplanes going over as, for example, Israel was able to pull off in Operation Orchard. So what I am getting at is be careful of steering Cyber Command more and more towards civilian roles. It may lead us to success in non-war but set us up for a fall in real war.

General ALEXANDER. I just want to add some clarity to that to make sure that, at least from my perspective, you understand because where you can get commercial industry to help is to do their part. That is the war game and the effort. But Cyber Command and our Defense Department cannot work without the energy sector. If that is shut down, we got a problem. Our Defense Department needs to defend the nation in this area. I am not proposing that they go in and prop up any energy company or any of these. Help them build the right cybersecurity so that we know they can defend themselves and call for help when they need it, and then push that out beyond the boundary.

But I think our Defense Department has to think more comprehensively of this whole thing. I agree. Going after all targets and stuff is part of it. But my concern is the easy thing, if I were a bad guy, I would just go after our infrastructure. I would take it out before you could respond. That is what the Chinese approach to warfare is. So I think we have to put all that on the table, wargame it, and then ensure we have it correct.

Senator SULLIVAN. Thank you.

Thank you, Mr. Chairman.

Chairman MCCAIN. Senator Ayotte?

Senator AYOTTE. I want to thank all of you for being here. Appreciate it.

I wanted to follow up, General Alexander, on something that you had in your prepared statement, and you wrote that Russia's intervention in Ukraine and in Syria—the Syrian conflict are just the start of a potential series of actions that seek to reshape the international environment. So I wanted to get your assessment based on all your experience of what comes next with Moscow and what should we be doing to respond.

General ALEXANDER. Well, my greatest concern is eastern Ukraine. I think everything that is going on is for Putin to get more closure on eastern Ukraine where the weapons platforms that he really cares about are created. I think he wants control of that. I think by pushing what he has done, he is going to continue to go for that. There is nothing that I have seen that would indicate he is going to stop from doing that, and I think he will lie. He will do everything he can and then help make that happen.

Syria is a great way to push—you know, think of it as a faint. He can accomplish some real objectives there between Iran, Syria, and Russia, and he is doing that by helping to shape what he thinks are the best proxies for Russia, Syria and Iran, in the region. So he wins twice there. It takes our focus off eastern Ukraine—people are still dying there—and focuses everybody on Syria. I would not be surprised if over the next 6 months we see some more action in eastern Ukraine at the same time.

With respect to Syria, what I am really concerned about is the tension it creates up. We get to a point where we have to fire back against Russia or Iran for their actions in Syria. If we do that, I think we are going to see their response in cyber. I really do because there is no way Iran can come after us. They can launch terrorist attacks. We have been fairly good at stopping those, but they can hit us with cyber. It goes back to what is a credible deterrence. What happens if they change their approach from disruptive attacks against the financial sector to destructive against the financial and the energy.

Senator AYOTTE. So I guess I would—anyone who wants to comment on this. But as I hear you discuss this, I think if we let him continue to do this without any response, as far as I can see, does this not almost become a fait accompli, which we could see ourselves headed in this direction which is going to require—you know, put us in a more dangerous situation? If you were advising right now the President, what would you tell him to do to respond to Putin?

Mr. CLARK. I would say refocus back on Ukraine. So Syria is obviously a very dynamic and difficult situation, but Ukraine is a situation where we have a friend of the United States, not an ally, but a partner that is under threat and attack by Russia and providing the Ukrainians the capability to better defend themselves in the electromagnetic spectrum, as well as in cyber, would be really important to giving them the capability to defend themselves and disrupt the Russian attempts to gain more territory. That would force Putin to now refocus his effort back onto that and make a determination as to whether he is going to be resolved and continue in Ukraine or if he is going to eventually recede. But right now, because we have not been focused on it, he is able to continue to accrete influence without any counter.

General ALEXANDER. If I could. I agree. I think our vital interests in Eastern Europe and in the Middle East are at risk. I think we have already had some outcomes of the Iranian deal. I think having some deal with Iran to stop nuclear weapons is important, but we lost some of our allies in doing this. Losing those allies is something we cannot afford to have happen. So I think we have to step back and say what is our strategy for both. We are going to have to deal with both at the same time. In the Middle East, we need our allies to know we are going to stand beside them. It is the same thing in eastern Ukraine because everybody is looking at it. They say you have made all these declarations about NATO about you are going to be there for us. So what happens? Are you going to be there?

At times, unintentionally our actions may look like we are not. What I am concerned about when you talk to Saudis, the Israelis, and others, they think hold it. Are you here with us or are you with Iran? What is your objective? I think we have to clarify that. Our Nation needs to let our allies know we are there for them. I think that is the first and most important thing we should do, and we should discuss with them how we are going to stop issues in the Ukraine with NATO and what we are going to do in the Middle East to shore up our allies there.

Senator AYOTTE. Does anyone want to add to that?

Dr. SINGER. I would just add that the last several decades of U.S. foreign policy strategy, defense strategy has been focused on the challenge set of networks of individuals, criminals, insurgents, terrorists and the problem set of failed states. Moving forward, we are going to have to recognize that whether it is Russia or also China, we have a return to great state competition, and what that means is that when we look at certain areas, we need to look at it through a lens of not just the failed state but proxy warfare as well. I think we are seeing certain echoes of that and we are going to be able to learn the lessons from the past of what does and does not work in proxy warfare and reframe our approaches along those lines. On top of this is focusing on how do you keep a lid—how do you win a competition, but also keep a lid on it from escalating.

Senator AYOTTE. Thank you all. Appreciate it.

Chairman MCCAIN. General, just to follow up on your comment to Senator Ayotte, you say we would have to take some actions to reassure our allies or other nations in the region in the Middle East. What actions would those be?

General ALEXANDER. I think we need to reach out to Saudi Arabia, United Arab Emirates, Kuwait, Jordan, and Egypt and sit down with them and say we are here. I think some of things that we ought to talk about is——

Chairman MCCAIN. We say that all the time, by the way.

General ALEXANDER. You know, when you look at it, when you look at Egypt, perhaps some of the best comments I have heard on a strategy for Egypt was, well, how do you get them stability. How do you get them security? You got to have energy to growing jobs. You got to give these guys jobs. 24 percent unemployment is really bad for us. It is bad for the world. How do we help get the Middle East in place? They have enough money to do it. We have the expertise to help them get there. I think we have got to look at the security, the stability, the energy sector, and the jobs, the economic development for the Middle East to get them to a place where they can be looking forward to their future versus fighting all these issues that we are seeing with radical Islam. So I think a comprehensive program like that, led by our country and others in the Middle East, is a step forward and let them know that we are going to be there not just for a couple hours but for the next several decades.

Chairman MCCAIN. Right now, the Egyptian regime is becoming more and more repressive. 45,000 people in prison, no semblance of any real progress on a number of areas which are in contradiction to our fundamental principles.

General ALEXANDER. This is a tough area. I have been to Egypt several times, and there is no good solution without economic growth. So I guess the question, Chairman, is how do we help them get out of this because in my dealings with our counterparts, they understand and want to do it. How do you get there? There is so much tension in that region. If we do not help them get to economic growth, what they are going to have is continued failed states, and with those failed states, now we got—it is just another one. So it seems to me at some point we have got to come up with a strategy that counters that. I personally believe that that is some way of developing their economies.

Chairman MCCAIN. Dr. Singer, I have your book on my desk admittedly in a pile of books on my desk. I will move it to the top of the pile. The next time I encounter you, I will be able to give you a vigorous critique of the thesis that you espouse in that book. Congratulations on its success.

Mr. Scharre, thank you for your articulate answers to the questions.

Mr. Clark and General Alexander, a special thanks to you for your past service but also it will be the intention—and we do work on a bipartisan basis, as you know, with this committee—to start looking at the follow-on to the cyber legislation that we just passed through the Senate. We will be calling on all of you as we move forward with that effort. I think you would agree that additional legislation is necessary. Would you agree with that, General?

General ALEXANDER. I do, Chairman.

Chairman MCCAIN. Thank you.

Jack?

Senator REED. Mr. Chairman, this was an extraordinarily insightful panel. I am not surprised. You chose wisely, a West Point graduate whose fleet commander shaped his life. You have a submarine officer. You have an Army Ranger, and you have a graduate of Harvard University. So good job, Mr. Chairman.

Chairman MCCAIN. The hearing is adjourned.

[Whereupon, at 11:46 a.m., the hearing was adjourned.]

○